JANE M. CHAMBERLAIN

TAROT
THE ULTIMATE GUIDE TO TAROT CARD READING

Descrierea CIP a Bibliotecii Naționale a României
JANE M. CHAMBERLAIN
Tarot The Ultimate Guide to Tarot Card Reading / Jane M. Chamberlain. – Bucharest: Editura My Ebook, 2020
ISBN 978-606-983-580-7

JANE M. CHAMBERLAIN

TAROT
THE ULTIMATE GUIDE TO TAROT CARD READING

My Ebook Publishing House
Bucharest, 2020

Table of Contents

Chapter 1. An Historical Overview 7

Chapter 2. Intuition and the Tarot 11

Chapter 3. Getting Started - Clearing your Tarot Deck and Space 16

Chapter 4. The Major Arcana 24

Chapter 5. The Minor Arcana 59

Chapter 6. Cups 86

Chapter 7. Pentacles 117

Chapter 8. Swords 149

Chapter 9. Conclusion - An Easy Spread To Get You Started ………………………………………… 179

Chapter 1

An Historical Overview

When we think of tarot cards we think of the occult, mysticism and divination. Well the truth of the matter is that the original tarot cards were actually used to play games with. The basic rules for playing the tarot games appear in a Italian manuscript of Martiano da Tortona dating back to 1425 with the Italian wealthy classes. It is a fact that the beginnings of the tarot deck started in the 15th century in Italy between 1420 and 1440. There is no substantial evidence linking the tarot at that time to ancient Egypt although certain Egyptian symbols are present on the cards. But, we can to take account the history between Rome and Egypt in deciding how much Egyptian influenced these cards actually contain. This would be based on ones historical perspective even if the jury in some cases are decided that there is no proof of such a relationship.

Created as a game for the nobles; the 22 cards we refer to as the "Major Arcana" was a lavish hand painted set of cards for the Italian nobility to entertain themselves with. This is not the same deck of cards we know today as playing cards which date back to the Chinese and the 12th century. Those cards were created at that time to entertain the Chinese King's concubines. This origin of playing cards is a credible story as to the creation of cards because the Chinese also created paper which the cards were made of.

The three decks from the Italian Nobility in 1440 called the Visconti Trumps are the ones by historical consensus that are regarded as the ancient elders of the Tarot as we know them today. Like all playing cards at the time these early decks had number cards 1 to 10 in 4 suits and the court cards page, knight, queen, king and 22 cards not belonging to any suit. These cards bore symbolic pictures with subjects like the Pope, the Emperor, The Wheel of Fortune, The Devil and the Moon. We recognize these same names in the Major Arcana portion of the tarot decks we use today.

The tarot cards were used to play a new card game at that time called "Triumphs". It was similar to bridge with the 22 cards without suits serving as the "trump" cards. The trump cards out ranked the other cards in the deck. This card game was extremely popular among the ruling and upper classes in Italy; spreading quickly through Northern Italy to the East of France. As the card game spread to other countries in Europe changes were made to the pictures as the ranking of the trump cards which bore no numbers. As time ensued the card game spread to Northern Sicily, Austria, Germany and the lower geographically countries.

There is evidence however that in the 16th century the tarot was used to compose poems in which personality characteristic descriptions were taken from the tarot. Poets would use the titles of the trump cards to create flattering verses to describe the ladies in the court. In one specific case in 1572 a poem related to a person's fate. It is noted that the use of the tarot cards for divination purposes dates back to 1750 where the divinatory meanings and uses of that deck was completely different as it is used today. Although in 1589 there was a case implying witchcraft and the use of the Tarot cards there is no other real written evidence of its occult use until the 18th century. It was not until really the 18th century that the tarot was viewed as having mystical and spiritual/occult meanings. But keep in mind that although it wasn't the norm in terms of card usage; ordinary playing cards were associated with divination and the occult as far back as 1487. There is concrete evidence the early divinatory meanings were given to the tarot as far back as 1700's in Bologna.

The first detailed reference of the Trump cards of the tarot was in a sermon. It was given by a Franciscan friar between 1450 and 1470 who states the Trumps were devised by the Devil himself. The use of the cards were condemned and the Devil is credited with the final triumph of the trumps. He contended that the Devil wins through the loss of souls in the card game.

The word "Tarot" is argued about whether or not it derived from Egypt, Hebrew or Latin as an anagram originally. Well, historical finds imply it comes from the first word "tarocchi" which is plural; or "tarocco" which is singular for the game of triumphs or trumps 100 years after the first deck emerged. No one really knows why the word tarot appeared but they do know the Germans called the deck tarok and the french tarot.

In terms of ancient historical association of the tarot and its history; Antoine Court de Gebelin in the 18th century in France became convinced that the tarot deck had a connection to Egypt based on its picture symbolism. In his book **"Monde Primitif"** he alluded to the fact that the pictures in the Tarot are from the ancient books that were not burned in Egypt. He also felt that there were secrets that had to be decoded in those pictures. Soon after everyone was viewing the tarot as a card system deep with hidden meanings.

The secret history of the tarot was again stirred up by the notion that the originator of the secrets was a god known as "Thoth" also called Hermes Tresmagistus. Modern occult tarot began in 1781 when the same swiss clergymen and Freemason Antoine Court de Gébelin, published a speculative study *"Le Monde Primitif"*, which included the religious symbolism of the tarot. He wrote that the symbolism of the Tarot de Marseille contained symbols representing Isis and Thoth. He further said that the word Tarot came from the Egyptian word "Tar" meaning royal and "Ro" meaning road. He concluded that the Tarot was meant as the royal road to wisdom. He also asserted that it was indeed the gypsies who were descendants from Egypt who used the cards for divination first and were the first as a nomadic group to introduce the cards to Europe. Although the later Egyptologists could not find anything to substantiate this it has remained solid as part of the Tarot legacy.

In 1781 the Comte de Mellet wrote a short article on tarot in published in Court de Gébelin's *Le Monde Primitif.* He was the first to write that there was a connection between Hebrew letters and the cards. In the 19 century the famous occultist Eliphas Levi developed a relationship between the Kabbalah and the Tarot. The Kabbalah is what is referred to as Hebrew mysticism. Now, this fueled the idea that the Tarot originated in Israel and contained the wisdom of the Tree of Life from the Kabbalah. This idea brought the 78 cards together into a uniform key to the mysteries and was passed on to the English speaking world through the Hermetic Order Of The Golden Dawn. The Theosophical Society, the Hermetic Order of the Golden Dawn, the Rosicrucians, the Church of Light, and the Builders of the Adytum (B.O.T.A.) all secured the Tarot's position in the 19th and 20th centuries as a viable form of divination.

It was author Edward Waite who was accredited with the Renaissance of the Tarot in the 20th century. It was he who commissioned Pamela Coleman Smith to create what he called the "Rectified Tarot ." He, himself being a member of secret societies also collaborated with one of his brothers known as a revered mystic. The man whose last name was Rider gave way with Waite to the Rider-Waite's 1910 Tarot Deck. This deck has become the worldwide standard Tarot deck. It was and still is the most popular deck to date because of its rich symbolism and ease to interpret.

Chapter 2

Intuition and the Tarot

We all have a certain degree of what is called intuition. This may or may not include being psychic as well. Intuition is our innate abilities to sense things in the world around us. It is our instinctive or unconscious knowing that has nothing to do with our cognitive abilities of reason and logic. Intuition is a gut instinct that we feel regardless of what we are logically supposed to feel or not based on a specific situation. It lets us know when there is danger or what kind of people are around us. It is our innate inner sense we have that switches on for certain situations we may deal with when logic isn't the way to assess it. For example; a person may appear to be nice but out intuition may sense otherwise. So, in that case it is wise to keep on guard until the person proves if they are really nice or not. It may be that the person even seems nice but something isn't quite right with them; so our gut tells us to be on guard something is wrong. That is intuition. It's that feeling we get in situations where our logic isn't able to address or assess a situation and the feeling is telling us what's happening.

Being psychic is the apparent sensitivity to things beyond what is accepted as the normal range of perception. It can take many forms. Hollywood and the media always make it appear as some extra ordinary ability to bend objects and move concrete material with our minds. Although these phenomena do happen and people are gifted with that ability; not every psychic can do that. Some people have the gift to hear things, some see things, some can channel in the spiritual realm. All these I mentioned and other things too are associated with being psychic. Just like intuition; a person who is considered psychic has the abilities to innately sense things. Not all psychics execute their psychic abilities the same way. For instance, some psychics possess such abilities as clairvoyance (to hear things spiritually) and others may be telepathic (able to read or hear what a person is thinking or saying non verbally). Others may have paranormal aptitudes (example; able to bend objects or move them with their minds) or supernatural inclinations (example: to see and feel beyond the normal range of logic by communicating with spirits). One can have intuition and not be psychic and one can be both psychic and an intuitive.

To read the tarot it isn't necessary to be psychic but it is important to tune in to our intuitions. What is interesting however is the more we use our intuitions the more we open up our senses and have psychic moments as a result. Each tarot card has a standard meaning but the difference between a good tarot card reader and an ordinary one is how developed their intuitions are. An intuitive tarot card reader will use their senses and gut feelings as well as the literal interpretation of a card to get the full essence of the cards meaning. Like everything else in life the more we use our intuition the sharper it becomes. The stronger our intuitions develop the more accurate our readings become. Tarot cards are tools that help focus the intuition for those with intuitive skills. Some people have intuition as a gift others may have to work harder to open that part of themselves in order to have a little intuition. Many times those with strong intuitions to the point of being psychic may have had it in their families and it is passed along from generation to generation.

Many people that are not opened to the idea of the Tarot and intuition dismiss the idea of reading with the cards as a cheap parlor trick. The truth is that most people have a misconception of what a reading is. It's the intuitive gifts that the reader has and how he or she applies them to the cards that makes a reading effective. Most people who read cards are already intuitive to an extent from very early on in their lives which is what made them gravitate to the tarot in the first place. The tarot are not magic in and of themselves when you take the cards out the box. It's the persons energy that is used to create that for lack of a better word a "magical" interaction between himself and the cards. It's the persons connection to the cards their intuition and their interpretation that makes the magic happen during a reading.

Like there are many types of card readers; there are many tarot decks to choose from. What happens is when a person goes to buy a tarot deck it is usually the artwork that draws them to that deck. A person will read effectively if they can connect to the artwork on the cards. This is because the artwork gives the person a feeling based on what the pictures mean to them. For instance, someone with an American Indian spirituality may gravitate towards those decks influenced by the American Indian people both spirituality and culturally because they can identify with the artwork. The symbolism therefore in the cards is enhanced by the affinity the person has to the art work both culturally and spiritually.

The other thing that is important for that magical connection to the cards is the life force energy in our bodies. It's that energy in our bodies that circulates through our being and connects us to our spiritual essence. Life force is what gives us a will, a vibrancy and a spiritual connection to things outside of ourselves also. This same energy is released when we touch the cards. Our energy is imparted into the cards by just putting our hands on them. When we use the cards in a reading our energy flows into the cards from our hands because we consciously direct our focus to the cards for a reading. Different readers use this energy different ways. Some will actually let the client touch their cards in order to feel the person they are reading's energy; while other readers won't because they do not want to mix their energy with the people they are reading. I myself do not let people touch my cards but I have friends who are gifted readers who do. It's up to how we the reader decides to work with the energy we have as well as the energy of the person who is being read.

When we choose the cards for a spread; (and this is true particularly seasoned readers) the cards embark an energy through our hands and tell us when to stop shuffling and or when to throw a card on the table. This is how it works for me and I know it works for other readers as such. There are those readers who will use the other persons energy and have them shuffle and pick the cards for their reading. In either case it is that same energy that drives the person to pick and shuffle the cards for the message they are about to receive.

The other interesting thing is that the symbolic meaning of cards vary among readers. It depends on how their intuitions interpret and relate to a particular card. For example, the death card for one reader may literally mean someone is going to pass; and for others it may mean the end of a particular period for a person in their life. So if someone goes to a reader and sees the death card it doesn't necessarily mean someone is going to die. It may mean the end of a relationship or lifestyle or that someone needs to completely change their life. It is all about how the reader connects to the images in the cards and senses how it relates to the person being read.

When one first starts to read the tarot there may be confusion about the interpretation of a card. This is when one's intuition really is asked to work. When this happens it's good to focus all your attention and energy on that card and ask your intuition to tell you what that card is saying. Envision it in your mind's eye and the scenario it conjures in your mind's eye. In this way it can help give you clarification to understand what message is being given by that particular card.

This is also a good way to develop your intuition in relation to reading the cards. You start by getting the traditional standardized meaning of a card and then ask your inner self, your intuition what does it mean. In this way you start to internalize the energy of the cards and mesh it with your intuition. This serves two purposes it helps you memorize each card by a standard meaning and then helps you develop your intuition as to what that card means to your senses. Note the feeling you get when you do this with each card because the feeling you get is the energy that that card draws on. This is what makes the difference between anyone reading cards and a good reader. A good reader is in tune to their energy; the connection they have with the cards and their intuition. These two elements energy and intuition are what goes into the cards from the reader to give a clear and accurate reading.

There are those readers who are also channelers and use spiritual guides to help them with readings. These are for the most part people who have intuition and then have a spiritual component on some level in which their psychic ability is able to work in the spiritual realm. These are those tarot readers who ask their guides to come in to help them when they do consultations. A guide is a spiritual entity that will help them with their readings. They may talk to them, they may guide their hands or they may actually enter the reader. You do not have to have this ability to read cards. This is a different aspect of a gift that I am not going to focus on in this book. I myself have guides who work through my hands, but it is not an essential for reading the tarot. What is important is that you are opened enough to let your intuition work for and with you when you interpret the cards and their meanings. I am an intuitive spiritualist. I have never took lessons and don't have the patience to read books on all the symbolism and details of the tarot cards in depth like some many do. My point is whatever works for you; take the basics and run with it to read the cards to the best of your ability.

Chapter 3

Getting Started - Clearing your Tarot Deck and Space

So you just got your new deck of tarot cards. They are still in the box. There is a process called clearing the deck that tarot readers do before they start to use the cards. This is done to clear any negative energy from the deck as well as to start to impart your own energy on the new deck. There is no one way to clear a tarot deck.

When you get a new deck of tarot cards it is recommended that they are spiritually prepared and cleansed so you can conduct readings more effectively. You can clear a tarot deck several ways. Clearing is a way to spiritually clean and prepare the cards for use. Many readers also cleanse their spiritual space and objects in the room they conduct readings in very much in the same manner. You can also clear the reading space, table and objects you use to read with to remove any negativity as well. The idea is you want to work with a card deck and space that is clean spiritually so that the readings aren't clouded with negative debris from other things. Spiritual cleanliness is next to whatever idea of godliness one has. When you clear your tarot cards you remove any traces of negative or blocking energy so you can use them to the best of your abilities with clean and positive energy.

Many people do spiritual preparations like clearing the space and cards of negativity before they begin to read a client in addition to their initial clearing. They also may do little cleanings after readings as well to make sure if there was any negativity from the reading that it is removed. Some people clear their cards after every reading some don't. They may do it periodically like on a specific day at a specific time. It doesn't matter which way you decide to clean them after the initial clearing. Go with how you feel and what gives you the best energy. Also by keeping cards and space spiritually cleansed it helps eliminate false and inaccurate readings. You won't have left over energy from the previous readings this way. The tarot cards are a form of divination. All forms of divination require energy. When you clean your cards and space you are ridding them of the energetic "residue" that accumulates from reading others or using the cards all the time. This is even more important if you are the type of reader who allows others to handle your cards. Reading different people constantly; and things like giving a reading that had bad or negative energy attached to it would be an adequate reason to make sure your cards are cleared. The cards accumulate energy which is the reason for spiritual cleaning. Clearing the cards and the area is like breathing clean air on them.

Some people can read without doing anything to a deck, but most people want to put their own energy into the deck instead of just taking them out of the box and beginning. When you clear a deck you are also charging it with your energy as you begin to use it, by removing any other influences on the cards. Clearing the deck also blesses the deck with your spiritual energy. Before I actually give you some simple techniques here is a list of all the main ways one can cleanse a tarot deck and the space you use to read with:

1. Prayers, Invocations, Vigils
2. Singing, Chanting or Music
3. Ritual Silence
4. Creating an alter, placing statues, flowers, pictures, a glass of water, material
5. Using A Power Name

6. Incense, Smoke and Smudging (including some people burn objects)
7. Special Gestures and Offerings, moving within or outside a circle, exchanging gifts (some people may symbolically know something down or break something)
8. Lighting candles or burning a fire
9. Fasting or Feasting on special foods such as eating a special thing or drinking a specific herb or tea
10. Using power objects such as crystals or putting on any ritual amulets or talisman or religious or spiritual jewelry such as beads
11. Burying or Unburying
12. Tying or Untying
13. Washing your hands
14. Breathing techniques
15. Shuffling

Most people begin a clearing of the cards and the space they are going to use by invoking good energy to assist them. They ask the good energy to clear the tarot deck and space; and also ask the good energy to give the deck and space a positive charge. The good energy can take the form of what you perceive as good energy; be it a spirit guide, a departed ancestor, white light, whatever does it for you. Some people ask for Gods light and intervention; based on what God means to them. The point is they use whatever they feel is a good and positive force for them to clear any negative or blocks from the cards and space. Many readers also consecrate of dedicate their cards to the use of good when they clear their space and tarot deck as well.

Here is a simple invocation to clear the " deck" or space to start. When using it for your space you substitute the word space for deck.

It takes the form of a consecration of the deck in the name of good energy.

"I consecrate this deck to bring Light where there is Darkness.

I consecrate this deck for guidance and wisdom for myself and others for the higher good for all concerned.

I consecrate this deck to enlighten myself and those concerned.

May all who use and touch this deck know the love of Spirit and drawn into the light of Spirit.

I dedicate this deck to serve others with spiritual growth, for wisdom, knowledge, and to bring peace to all those who seek its wisdom.

I dedicate this deck to the development of my intuition so that I may be a source of guidance to others".

You may add any words you wish or change any of them to fit the energy you are using as well as your feelings. This is a non denominational invocation for universal good energy. It is a form of consecration to make the deck of pure good light energy. When we consecrate something we make it holy to ourselves be it a person, place or thing. By doing this we are removing all the negative energy things accumulate. Your intention is very important for doing clearing and cleansing. You want to have a clear head and heart free from any negative intent and thought when you do this. Sincerity is the first element that goes into being of pure heart and mind. You may also want to thank all those energies that are assisting in the cleansing also. When we give thanks we bring thanks in our lives which brings blessings.

There are two main ways people proceed while invoking the good energy of the universe to their decks and spaces is by either shuffling the cards while they say the invocation or putting the cards in numerological order before they say the invocation. You can do what you prefer. You may decide to do neither and just place your hands on the cards or put the deck of cards up to your heart. Tarot cards can be blessed in many ways. You don't have to use the invocation I wrote above that's just an idea. Any prayer that has meaning to you is fine. A mantra even works if your intention is clear and positive. The main point is to put your cards in touch with a higher good with which it is empowered with.

You can then go on to use incense, smudging whatever you want to do to clear the air and the cards. You can pass the cards through the smoke. Some readers use oil like lavender and drop a few drops on the cards. Some may sprinkle the cards with salt. They may rap them hard against the table. Some even fling them across the room to rid them of negativity. Whatever works for you and your beliefs.

When this is done It can be wrapped in a silk cloth or put in a bag just for the cards. I keep mine in a wooden box from my mother. Some people sleep with them under their pillows.

People do things from Reiki to keeping the cards clean; to very involved rituals. Some put a crystal on the deck to keep it charged and cleared when they are not in use. These are just a few basic ideas on how to clear your tarot card deck. There are however also very involved rituals tarot card readers use but I did not include them in this book.

Some tarot card readers choose to do elemental clearing. This means using an element or elements to clear their cards with. In this case they work with one of the four elements to clear their deck. The elements they use are Earth, Fire, Water and Air. Here are some basics if you choose to clear your cards by the elemental method.

Earth Element Clearing

These are some methods you can use to clear your cards with things considered of the earth element.

1. You can actually bury your deck in the silk or bag in dirt, sand or salt for 24 hours.

2. You can spread the deck in a fan shape on a table with a cloth under it and sprinkle sand and or salt on them for one to two minutes. Discard the sand and salt afterwards. You can also make a powder by crushing dry herbs and then adding the salt and/or sand if you wish. You can also just use the herbs. Some suggested herbs are Basil, Lavender, Rosemary, Sage and Thyme. You can use herbs based on ones cultural affinity too. I like the herbs Yerba Buena (Mint) and Abre Camino (road opener) with Basil (Albacca)

3. Rub your deck with either sand or salt for a few minutes

4. Sleeping on the deck either under your pillow or mattress over night.

Water Element Clearing

1. Sprinkle the cards lightly with water and then wipe them off.

2. Mix the water with salt and then sprinkle and wipe (you can use a teaspoon of salt to a cup of water)

3. You can use a consecrated water like holy water to sprinkle and wipe the cards with

4. You can use herbal teas or infusions to sprinkle the cards with and then wipe (you can use the same herbs as the earth element either fresh or dry and boil)

5. Expose the cards to moonlight, make sure they are in a safe protected spot for half the night

Cleansing With The Fire Element

1. Pass the cards through a flame of a candle.(white candle) Don't burn yourself

2. Put the cards on a table with a lighted candle in front of them for about 5 minutes

3. You can place the deck near an oil burner with some sort of blessing oil of your choice, incense or the smudge stick for about 5 minutes

4. Leave the cards in the sun for about half a day

Cleansing With The Air Element

1. Passing the deck 5 to 7 times over burning incense
2. Smudge your deck with sage or herbs
3. Breathe deeply on the deck three times...slowly and deeply
4. Place the deck near playing music for one hour

There are those people who use the elements with elemental symbols based on their belief systems. I choose to remain non denominational for the purposes of this book.

There is a little "elemental ritual" you can do that is non denominational that you may use when consecrating you cards. You light a charcoal or incense and place it in the east direction of your table. You put a lit white candle in the south direction. You then put a glass of water in the West direction and a dish of salt in the North. Place the deck in the middle. Put a pinch of the salt in the water then pick up the cards fan them out and place back saying as you sprinkle the salt water that you are purifying these cards with water and earth. Then take the cards and pass them through the incense and say you are purifying them with air and fire. You can leave the cards in the center until the incense and the candle go out and then put them in the cloth, bag or wooden box you have to keep them in.

These are all just a few ideas you can do to cleanse and clear your deck. There are many ways to do so. One final way to clear a deck after a very negative reading or encountering negative energy would be to put it in a leak proof container and bury them for a few days. In this way the earth absorbs the negativity. Otherwise, when you use your cards after the initial cleansing; while shuffling them before you use them daily envision that the shuffle is cleansing them with water to remove the debris from earlier use. You can occasionally fan them out for this purpose also. Cleanse and clear your cards as often as you feel you need to.

Readers will smudge their cards and reading areas between readings and keep crystals on top of their decks when not in use all in an effort to keep the cards and space spiritually clear. Some tarot readers like to reorganize the deck literally by placing the cards in a particular direction and order between readings. Others may clap their hands and or use a noise such as a bell, a gong or chimes to break stagnant energy surrounding them and their cards. There are those readers who may use visualization and imagine white light as in reiki around their cards to clear them of negativity. Some cross their wrists over the deck and quickly uncross them to break any dark energy on the cards before they begin to do a reading. They also may use the knuckle of their non dominant hand and hit the cards hard imagining a white light emanating from that hand through the cards to cleanse them. The reader then picks them up puts them to their heart and imagines gold light embracing the cards. They will either pray or say a mantra to rededicate good energy to their cards. The point is there are countless ways to clear and charge the cards. The main thing is to find what feels right for you and use what works for you.

Chapter 4
The Major Arcana

The "Major Arcana" are considered the heart of a tarot deck. Also known as the "Trump cards" there are 22 of them. They do not have suits attached to them like the rest of the tarot deck. It is human life and experience from birth through death that is represented in the Major Arcana portion of the tarot deck. It symbolizes the physical, spiritual, intellectual and emotional aspects related to man and the universe.

The trumps includes archetypes of people in its 22 cards. For example some of the aspects of the cards in the major arcana may relate to warmth and nurturing as with a mother figure or strong and commanding as an authoritative figure, as is a traditional religious figure or a mystical personality; these are just some of the types of people it can represent. The archetypes in the Major Arcana are however indicative of real people whether figuratively or actually in someone's life.

Each card of the 22 Major Arcana depict a scene which contains symbolic elements in it. In many decks each card is numbered from 0 to 22 in Roman numerals with a word describing each card. There are some decks however with no numbers or word on top to describe the card. Some decks only have pictures. The earliest decks had no numbers or words as well; probably because most people were illiterate. In the early days the cards were not in a standard numbered order as they are today.

The pictures on the major arcana are steeped with symbolism. Major Arcana cards are related to thing regarding one's higher purpose or a deep significance affecting one's life. They depict a person's journey in life particularly in relation to personal development. As their numbers start at 0 to 22 it is the journey from innocence to wisdom. Some tarot scholars believe the sequence depicts the enlightenment one attains in one's lifetime. It is also intended to be a path of enlightenment for one to take as well as learning the meaning of one's true self. We see the first card the fool starting out in life with decisions and directions to make where he meets the magician who gives him an idea (card #1) and then we meet the high priestess etc. and so on down the line to 22. The Major Arcana focuses on our spiritual self but also gives us answers to things concerning our day to day lives like family, social relationships, jobs, finances and more.

The Major Arcana represents some aspect of the human experience we go through in our lives. It also looks at our spiritual journey here in our life, our hopes, dreams, fears, joys and sadness. When one starts their learning of how to use the tarot it is always suggested to familiarize yourself with the Major Arcana first. When you are comfortable with them they can help unlock the intuition you use for the divination of the Tarot.

When doing readings with the tarot deck you look at the card in the upright position and the reversed position. Depending on how the cards falls indicates if it is in a positive or negative aspect. Just because a card in itself is reversed does not make it negative. It depends on the cards imagery, its meaning and it relationship to the other cards in the spread. Like I said earlier in the book; people also use their own interpretations of the symbolism once they get an idea what the card represents as well.

For purposes of this book we are going to focus on the Rider Waite Deck. There are other decks you can work with and choose, I find this is the best for introducing someone with how to read the tarot. This is because there is so much information available for this particular tarot deck. The Major Arcana have been referred to as the 22 keys to life.

Here is a general divinatory description and meaning of each of the Major Arcana Cards:

0
The Fool
The Ruler: Air

The major Arcana Starts with the Fool. He is represented by the number zero. In medieval times he was the court jester. An innocent in god's eyes who said and did the most inappropriate things and got away with it. He chooses and does what he wants.

The Fool is the card of new beginnings and making choices. It represents unmolded potential which is neither good nor bad but contains both good and bad. The choice is the Fool's to make whether to go on the good path or bad. He is at a crossroads.

The Fool Upright

This represents the type of person who is unconventional and does not care or listen to what others have to say. The fool does what is comfortable to him. He does not hide from the light; he is like the light of an innocent child.

This card stands for new beginnings, new choices to be made, new experiences and a new path or direction one is thinking about taking.

It is also a path or choice that is filled with uncertainty. The Fool is a card of taking chances. The expression associated with the Fool card is "look before you leap."

It is also a card of a new life energy cycle. It is about energy, force, happiness and optimism. The Fool is about overturning the status quo of existing states of things by unexpected happenings. Innocence, naivety and spontaneity is also attached to the Fool. The Fool is the card indicating that important decisions have to be made.

Reversed

When the Fool is reversed it is advised not to take risks at this time. It is also advising against rash decisions, as well as impulsive actions and choices. Upside down the Fool represents being foolish, gambling, instability and wasting creative energy. When the Fool appears in reverse it is indicating that it is a bad time to make commitments and also indicates that this person likes to start things but never finishes what they start. It also points to a person who is constantly changing their environment and job.

I
The Magician
Ruler: Mercury

The number one is the number of creation and individuality. This is what "The Magician" is about; the power to transform through the use of his will. He takes the nothing like the Zero of the Fool and transforms it into the number one. He is the conduit of a higher power. The Magician is also an illusionist. Like all illusionists he can create an illusion of reality by the use of the sleight of hand and tricks. He is only confident in the skills he has in order to bring forth the results he wants. His real power comes from those sources outside of himself, just like in a magic show there are people behind the scenes to make it happen. Without the sources he too is powerless.

Magician Upright

When the Magician pops up it is warning about opportunity that we can have as long as we pull all the aspects in our life together to make it happen. It tells us the more prepared we are for the change the better it will be. It talks about the person mastering the material world. It's done through being organized, using creative action, self discipline, and a willingness to take risks.

This person has the gift of speech and to sway people. He or she has to recognize their potential and have the power to initiate things. They are witty and have very good communication abilities. This person can achieve anything they set out to do.

Magician Reversed

When the magician appears reversed this person is a bit of a perfectionist. They may appear outwardly to be able to handle any situation because they seem cool and calm; but inside they are indecisive and unprepared. They can use their gift of gab to manipulate and take advantage of people. It also indicates someone who abuses their power and uses it for negative purposes.

The magician reversed indicates someone who is confused and unorganized. They do not make decisive choices. They like to hesitate rather than choose. They are unable to properly utilize their time and talents. People who are represented by this card in this position are lacking inspiration and energy. They give up easily, have a poor self image and have poor coordination; and sometimes learning difficulties.

II
The High Priestess
Planet: Moon

The High Priestess is the symbol of spiritual enlightenment. She sits between a palm and pomegranate tree which are symbols of male and female energy. Her crown has the full moon and she represents every virgin goddess.

The High Priestess Upright

Along with spiritual enlightenment she also represents inner illumination and the link between that which is seen and unseen. She is the feminine form of balance and power. When she shows up in a spread she is telling us to use our intuition or that we have good intuition. The High Priestess also represents the unconscious mind and inner voice we have trying to give us a message. It is said when she appears hidden knowledge or information will be revealed or there is such information that is hidden that needs to come to the light. She represents unrevealed truth and hidden influences at work.

If she appears in a man's spread she represents the woman of his dreams. It's the love he has been hoping for. In a woman's spread she represents the virtues that the woman wishes for or has. In any spread she means something is yet to be revealed. That there may be duality and mystery in association with a situation or person. This card suggests hidden influences that affect the home and work of a person. It also represents a woman's influence.

High Priestess Reversed

In the reverse position the High Priestess means obvious knowledge and facts. It means any decisions you make will be based on facts and logic rather than intuition. It can indicate in this position the lack of balance and harmony due to insufficient foresight. It also indicates that the feminine or intuitive side of a person's personality may be repressed. If it's reversed in a woman's spread they have a problem coming to terms with another woman or themselves. It also means surface knowledge and or repression or ignorance of true facts and feelings. Sometimes it indicates being self centered and sensual pleasures depending what's next to it in a spread. Reversed it can also mean things and circumstances are not what they seem.

III
The Empress
Ruler: Venus

This card represents the personification of the Earth Mother. Her shield which is heart shaped has the symbol of Venus on it. The Empress is the Goddess of love and fertility. Some of the names she is known as is Venus and Aphrodite.

Empress Upright

The Empress upright represents fertility and bounty. Her power is that of creation. She creates life in all forms and ways. As an archetype she represents a mother. Motherhood, pregnancy and nurturing are the characteristics this card brings with it. She also represents everything created in nature. The Empress as with a mother also represents unconditional love. She represents abundance material wealth, creation infertility and in artistic expression. The Empress can also represent the security and stability that comes from years of a blissful marriage. When she shows up in a spread it can indicate a person who is over protective. She can also indicate a person who is gentle and loving, elegant and gracious. In a spread upright it can mean the birth of a child is on the way. It can also indicate that you need to be open to unconditional love. The Empress can also mean for those artistic types that they need to nurture and develop their artistic expression as in planting the seeds for a bountiful harvest. It is a card promoting well being and security. The person is creative in finances, love and parenthood. This card indicates a person who is maternal in nature as well as domestic stability. The Empress indicates achievement in goals and growth. Depending on the other cards around it can also mean a marriage.

Empress reversed

When she shows up reversed it indicates trouble in paradise; domestic disharmony. It can also indicate that the problem in the home is arising from infertility and or finances. The reversed Empress indicates a lack of affection either given or received and lack of achievement. It can indicate a creative block, problems in a relationship, an unwanted pregnancy or abortion, infertility, promiscuity or sterility. The reversed Empress can indicate poverty and trouble with children. When the Empress shows up reversed its time to think about what is causing problems in your home.

IV
The Emperor
Ruler: Aries

The Emperor represents power. The Magician has power through intellect, the High Priestess has power through knowledge, the Empress through love. The Emperor's power is through power period.

The Emperor Upright

This is a person that is in control. Nothing will stop him. He was born to lead and will dispose of anyone in his way. This card is one indicating success in a spread. If it's in a good position it can represent the attainment of goals and ambitions reached. As you see in the picture the Emperor has a commanding presence as he sits on his throne. The number of this card 4 represents stability and foundation. The Emperor represents domination of the material world. He is law and authority as an archetype. He can also represent a paternal figure and once again a powerful person. This card can also represent someone who is sexually controlled in their sex drive. People who have the Emperor as their personality card or show up in a spread as such; are competitive and forceful in how the execute things and how they develop them as well. This person is authoritative and the card can represent world power, structured and also governmental and corporate identities. Through their experience they have gained self control. These are very powerful people who can shoulder responsibilities. Their ambitions lead them to long term achievement.

The Emperor Reversed

When the Emperor is reversed it implies that the person is emotionally immature and unable to leave the nest. (He is a mama's boy) He cannot separate from his parents. In reverse this card represents a loss of control. It also shows that the person is inactive and doesn't take action but rather is passive on the sidelines. They either lost their position of authority or does not like authority at all. This includes a loss of authority in a governmental position or parental authority. Also they may not like the government or do not want to be a parent. This person is indecisive. There is weakness in his character. And he manipulates colleagues and friends alike. In reverse it can also mean an abuse of power.

**V
The Hierophant
Ruler: Taurus**

In some tarot decks the Hierophant represents the Pope. This is because this card represents the ruling power of religion and faith. It symbolizes the orthodox teachings that are palatable to the masses. This is in contrast to the High Priestess who only teaches those secretly who are initiated to her mysteries.

The Hierophant Upright

When this card turns up in a reading it indicates the person has a preference for a routine of ritual and ceremony. It represents spiritual power through an establishment. This is a card that symbolizes the church or a group belief system. It can also represent consensus of politics or public opinion. The Hierophant card indicates the person accepts authority. It's a card of conformity. It's about safety in numbers and social pressure. When this card pops up in a spread it indicates the person has a preference for ritual and ceremony. It also suggests the person needs approval from others. This card is showing the importance of conformity. This person may have a need to conform or is only happy when he has societal approval. It also represents formal education. This person is a seeker of knowledge and wisdom. They either give or get good sound advice. This person can be good at teaching and a constructive councilor. This also represents marriage and partnerships that are bound by morality. The Hierophant is about a world with law and order. For them the innocent citizen needs to carry identity cards. They prefer the illusion of security at the expense of freedom. If this card is in a good position or aspect in a spread it represents a good and secure reputation in society. It can also mean that this person has the ability to subvert and escape authority depending on the spread.

The Hierophant Reversed

If the Hierophant shows up in reverse it represents a person who is opened to new ideas and thinks outside of the box. He is a non conformist. It can represent a rebel, a hippie, an artist that colors outside of the lines. It also can indicate that the person is at the stage in their life where they need to do something completely different or outside of their own restrictions. On the other hand, when this card is reversed it can mean misleading and or bad advice, poor counsel, slander and propaganda. It's a warning to beware of first impressions. There is a distortion of the truth here. It is also a bad time to sign agreements, and represents misleading advertisements. This person is unconventional and does not have family values because he rejects them. It can also indicate a loss of public standing and the suppression of individuality by an establishment.

**VI
Lovers
Ruler: Gemini**

You can see in this card two lovers standing in harmony, nude meaning they hide nothing from one another. The picture itself in the card implies that someone has to make a decision to go for temptation or not. They know that to have success in their lives together that they have to balance the subconscious with conscious desires.

The Lovers Upright

When this card show up in a spread it tells us we have choices to make. It also tells us that we are human and struggle between sacred and promiscuous love. Because of these two things this card also represents the balance between our inner feelings and outer aspects of our lives. This card is also the card of harmony and unions. It tells us to choose with our heart and not with our intellects. The lovers card can also represent difficult choices that are not related to love. When we see this card it's about a test that we are going through in relationship to considering our commitments. It can represent a struggle between two paths, abstract thought and harmony, internal harmony and union between two people as well as second sight. The lovers indicates desire, a new lover, relationships, physical attraction, love, sex and commitment. This card is about duty versus our hearts desires. How the choice we make affects the rest of our lives. It also speaks of taking a risk that would lead to fulfillment and your hearts desires instead of playing the easy and safe route in love. It also says once the decision is made if you stay dutiful you will receive the same.

Lovers Reversed

When this card appears reversed it show us the possibility of a poor choice was made as well as quarrels and infidelity in a relationship. The reversed Lovers is telling us we need to stabilize our emotions. It implies we need to get in touch with our rational selves not our carnal selves. In this position it suggests lust, moral collapse, temptation, indecision, separation, a failed love affair, emotional loss. When it appears reversed lovers can mean an unhappy love relationship and you don't know what to do about it. There is contradiction, deception, duality and one's own internal conflict. It is telling of infidelity and romantic disturbances. It indicates the person is indecisive and postpones decisions on choices. It also warns that this is not the time to make final decisions on an important matter. Finally it also speaks of the fact that you are being untrue to your own morals.

VII
The Chariot
Ruler: Cancer

The Chariot is a card that tells of riding through our adversities victory. Like in ancient times when the gladiators fought for their lives in chariot races, the chariot means you are fighting your way through your own battles without giving up.

The Chariot Upright

When we see this card in a spread it is telling us that our conflicts are going to end in victory. It advises that sustained efforts and perseverance in a struggle results in you ultimately winning in the end. This card in a spread tells of your self reliance and belief in your own abilities. It can also represent unexpected good news as well as travel and change. Depending on where it shows up in a spread it could literally mean a new vehicle as in a car for you is on the way. When we see this card it's about triumph, movement, self belief, assertiveness and good news. You will overcome life's obstacles you are now facing. The person is decisive and ambitious when it comes to achieving the goals they have. The victory you earned is well deserved. You have undergone a period of struggle resulting in worldly success. It implies self control, effort and perseverance on behalf of the person. This card is about how one works within the boundaries their life has set upon them and builds a successful existence in spite of the boundaries.

The Chariot Reversed

When the Chariot shows up reversed it is telling of someone who is either influenced or themselves a bully, arrogant and selfish. It can represent frustrations due to things not turning out how one has thought they would. It also indicates delays of travel and plans depending on its position in the spread. It talks about how plans do not go well. This person has disregard for others, they are associated with envy and avarice. The Chariot reversed indicates the person has lost control in their life resulting in chaos because the person has a flaws in their personality. It talks of imbalance and also of destruction. Reversed, the Chariot warns of overwhelming ambition and high expectations. The card reversed depending on its position also talks about out dated ideas and traditions.

**VIII
Strength
Ruler: Leo**

This is a card of strength in all the ways the idea of strength is expressed by Man. It shows a man alongside a lion and both are in harmony indicating strength does not necessarily mean the display of brute force but rather a wise display of control and understanding the beast in us. The man in the picture is able to pet the lion indicate that strength involves the use of gentle encouragement to get the results needed in one's life.

Strength Upright

The card represents its name Strength. Not just in the physical sense; but also implies when it is in a spread upright that the person has the ability to cope with immense pressures, and will win as he fights through it to the end. If ill health has been an issue with the person at hand this card popping up indicates a speedy recovery. This card also suggests that if you have any unhealthy habits now is the time to stop them. Strength in a spread indicates triumph in all the main things in your life. You will win in the challenges facing your relationships or your career. It indicates that you can defend yourself against jealousy, ignorance and oppression. It talks about the person having courage and self control. This card signals that the person has the virtue of fortitude. He or she is determined. They also can control the passion of emotions against their basic instincts. They control both their strength and power. It talks of the person having energy, being generous, optimistic, showing resolve and reconciliation.

Strength Reversed

When we see Strength in reverse it implies the person is insecure and fearful. It tells of the person giving up due to being beaten by unfair means. Upside down Strength tells of a person who uses their power in a wrong way and there may be a defeat involved. There is a lack of will power here. The person feels inadequate about something. They also have a pessimistic attitude in regard to things going on around them or in their lives. There is a tendency with this person to surrender to unworthy impulses. The card talks about tyranny. Depending on the spread there is a concession involved in the situation. The person has an inability to act on things. In this position this card also talks about being warned not to miss opportunities that are available for the person. Also its telling the person not to give up when they are so close to the finish line.

IX
The Hermit
Ruler: Virgo

Just like a hermit secludes himself living a life of seclusion and cloistered away from the world so is the implications of this card when it falls in a spread. We see the lone hermit with a light to guide him. This is the light of mans spiritual self shining as he walks alone.

The Hermit Upright

When we see the Hermit card either the person is living as such or needs to take heed to the wisdom of the Hermit and slow down. When he appears in a reading he symbolizes the need for careful consideration of issues. It also implies that the person is in need of rest; including peace and quiet. If there is a health consideration the Hermit card is saying it is a time to rest and convalesce. This card represents introspection, solitude, the person is looking for inner and spiritual answers as guidance, advice either given by the person or taken and patience. The person is in need of caution and prudence as well as discretion in their lives. There is an inner calm here. This card in a spread can also indicate a need to reach one's inner resources. Depending where it is in the spread it can also mean Assimilation and planning. Counsel is either given or received to the person when we see the Hermit. This person is either a wise guide or spiritual mentor or has one. It is time to stand back and reflect on circumstances when this card shows up in a spread. The Hermit warns about making hasty decisions and recommends that if a decision is needed; make it only after taking some direction from a trusted source.

The Hermit Reversed

When we see the Hermit reversed it means this person is impatient and because he is it leads to bad decisions and in turn loneliness. It also implies that this person is arrogant and obstinate. The person is suspicious or creates suspicion with his behavior. He also refuses to heed advice to help him. Reversed depending where it comes in a spread can mean fear and folly as well. This person refuses counsel or assistance. He or she is immature. It indicates some sort of isolation from others. This person displays negative resistance to help. The persons suspicions of others is not grounded or sound with substantial reasons in relation to a person's motives. It implies imprudent actions or decisions. There is a continuation of unhealthy habits and lifestyle that is not productive. Depending on the spread and surrounding cards; the person relies on their own resources which are not adequate. Finally this persons obstinacy is foolish.

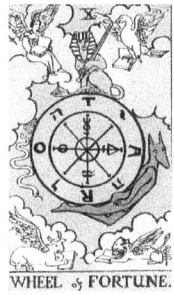

X
The Wheel of Fortune
Ruler: Jupiter

The Wheel of Fortune is a card Symbolizing Help from a higher source coming to aid the person. Like a circle the wheel is round representing when one cycle ends it goes right into the next as a circle continues. If we apply it to life when we are down on our luck the only way we can go is up. When we hit the bottom we have to come back up.

The Wheel of Fortune Upright

When the Wheel of Fortune appears it is telling us we are about to have a new life cycle. It portends good luck and fortune like the card's name. It also implies that it is fate that has brought this luck and fortune into one's life rather than by their own doing. This card heralds the end to current problems and rewards for past efforts. (It has a karma element in that case to it; fate is smiling on those who deserve it after they have paid for their trials and tribulations). It is a card of destiny, movement, vision, good luck, a new cycle and synchronicity. When it show up in a spread it is telling you of effortless success. It can also indicate unexpected good luck. It's a card of advancement. Positive upheaval as enforced changes for the better. Again it is a card of destiny in relation to ones Karma and a card indicating Karmic change.

The Wheel of Fortune Reversed

When the Wheel of Fortune is reversed we can expect some unexpected bad luck. It indicates that our fortune is turning in the opposite direction. It forebodes misfortune and unpleasant surprises when reversed. However many times the negative cycle it brings in reverse is temporary because the wheel always turns. Depending on where it shows up in reverse in the spread it can mean; obstacles, temporary bad luck, unpleasant surprises, unexpected interruptions, difficulties, delays and or a resistance to change. It also is a warning not to gamble when it's in reverse. Chance for loses.

XI
Justice
Ruler: Libra

The Justice card shows the sword and the balance scales being held by a person of royalty. This is a card of Justice and all its implications. That Justice is served through law and order for what is right as we see a sword. Balance is needed to serve justice, for when there is no balance injustice is in full swing.

Justice Upright

Like the card says when Justice shows up that's what it indicates. It indicates justice will be served. It can also represent that the person is fair or a fair decision will be made on behalf of the person or situation. It implies balance and equilibrium. Justice is a omen of good luck in relation to partnerships, businesses and legal dealings. The justice card can also signify the righting of a wrong that was done to you in the past or in your seeking justice for another. It is also a karmic card because those that do wrong are avenged by justice. It is a card also of rewards for past efforts. And, in some cases the person may not even know why they are being favored which is also a form of karma. When it shows up in a spread justice can imply arbitration, fairness and responsibility also. Depending on one's situation it can indicate amicable and favorable resolution of conflicts. It is a card representing triumph over bigotry and prejudice. Where this card shows up in a spread in relation to other cards can also mean legal action, litigation, contracts, settlements, divorce, and sometimes even marriage depending on the surrounding cards. This is only when marriage contracts like pre nups, legal documents or financial documents/statements are necessary to make the union happen. It is a card of clarity and a straightforward choice.

Justice Reversed

When Justice is reversed it represents injustice. It can also denote businesses that flounders and legal decisions that will not go your way even if you are morally right. It can also mean you are giving or receiving bad advice that will result in a bad judgment. Depending where it is in the spread also can mean prejudice, bias and inequality. It can indicate separations that are not yet ratified or legalized. Justice in reverse can mean delay, delay on judgments, imbalance, or an unfair judgment. There can be complicated negotiations taking place as well as confusion surrounding a legal matter or tax affair.

XII
The Hanged Man
Ruler: Neptune and Water

In the Hanged Man we see a man hanging by his foot from a tree. The man does not appear to be suffering but is in a position where he cannot move freely. This is a card of limitations which like the card seem beyond our immediate control, but like the hanged man we are forced by circumstance to accept this position. There is a temporary suspension of progress which is also a form the limbo that the Hanged Man can take as we see in his suspension from a tree.

The Hanged Man Upright

The hanged man is a card of self sacrifice. It can take the form of either material or emotional self sacrifice. This person may be in a state of limbo where like the picture portrays the man hanging from the tree experiencing a pause in life until someone or something is given up for greater gain. This card represents a trial of passage; and this is where the self sacrifice comes in. This card also has spiritual overtones in relation to one and self sacrificing themselves. It is also a card of adapting to changing circumstances. So in that regard depending where it shows in a spread it can mean transition, flexibility, rebirth, deliverance and release. It indicates there is devotion to a worthy cause. The Hanged Man can also imply flexibility of the mind and a willingness to make or adapt to changes depending on the cards around it. It indicates that there is a sacrifice being made now in order to reap benefits later. This card signals that there is a period of waiting for this person. When we see this card in a spread it indicates a sacrifice of one thing in order to gain something else. It is also a card of transformation. Changes are literally turned on the persons head. It can also indicate illness as well as stress and anxiety. The card indicates this is a time for patience and not to worry.

The Hanged Man Reverse

When we see the Hanged Man in reverse in a spread it is saying the person is selfish or is using emotional blackmail by playing the martyr. It also indicates there is a weakness with this person. Their weaknesses can lead them in the wrong direction both materially and emotionally resulting in missed opportunities otherwise. There is a lack of commitment to something. The person is preoccupied with material and selfish needs. Despite drawbacks they still prefer the status quo. It can indicate oppression depending on where it is in the spread as well as apathetic pursuit of goals. This person has the mentality "Better the Devil you know". There is a failure to act with an inability to move forward or progress. There is a stagnancy with this person.

XIII
Death
Ruler: Scorpio

Most people when they see this card in their spread get unnerved because they think death is announcing its coming. In actuality the death card rarely actually means death, it can but most of the times does not mean a physical death as we know it. When death shows itself in a spread its a definite ending and a definite new beginning. Death in the tarot card deck is about ultimate transformation. While the death card can mean shocking or unexpected changes and or events, it portends these things are being removed to clear a way for a brand new life. This card is about out with the old and in with the new; it's a complete transformation. Depending on the spread and surrounding cards it can mean sweeping changes, clearings and the beginnings of a new life. It represents that the change is a result of the underlying circumstances and this creates the transformation. It is a card of major change. It can also represent that a particular phase of life has played itself to the end, its purpose was served. The changes the death card talks of brings abrupt and complete overhauls of circumstances, ways of life and patterns of behavior do to past events and circumstances. It is also a card warning of altercations.

And finally yes for some readers death means a physical death. When this card appears it tests the person to see what they are made of.

Death Reversed

When this card appears reversed its telling you that you are resisting the inevitable changes that are needed in your life. It symbolizes stagnation when reversed. When the death card shows reversed its telling you that you are missing opportunities because of your refusal to let go to the situation. It can also represent fear of change in this position and a loss of a friendship. It shows in this position as a reminder that change is painful and unpleasant for this person. This person refuses to face their fears of change. Depending on where the card falls in the spread it can also mean the transition is agonizing for the person. In reversed the death card represents, inertia, lethargy as well as mental, physical and emotional exhaustion.

XIV
Temperance
Ruler: Sagittarius

When we see Temperance in a spread its about moderation. When we use moderation it will bring spiritual comfort. Temperance can also represent one's guardian angel looking over them. When this card appears it is saying this person either has or needs self control in their life. If they use control that will be able to handle volatile situations or a situation and come out successful for it. This card speaks of a harmonious relationship as well as peace and harmony in this time to be enjoyed. This card can also represent health, compromise and tranquility. Depending on the position it holds in the spread it can mean a good combination, cooperation and coordination of efforts. There is a innovation through the combination of either people or circumstances. It is also a card of diplomacy and successful business negotiations. There is a certain amount of maturity that the person has or needs in order to deal with something. This person has a placid, balanced temperament and good outlook. Literally this card means temperance in relation to harmony and balance. This card portends good management and the ability to adapt to changing circumstances.

Temperance Reversed

When temperance is reversed it is telling us that there is over indulgence, lack of foresight, impatience, conflict and quarrels causing domestic strife present. It warns that hasty decisions made out of impatience thwart the person's progress. Upside down temperance indicates and imbalance either with the person or situation they are in. This person or situation is heated and they or the person they deal with fly off easy because of it. There is poor judgment here as well as fickle decisions. Conflicting interests are present. There is physical stress with the person involved. Disagreements are prevalent. There is a restlessness and instability with the person or party involved. Depending on where it is in the spread it is saying that trying to combine too many things or the wrong elements in a short time span is not working.

XV
The Devil
Ruler: Capricorn

When we see the Devil card it is not necessarily pure evil as is Satan but more the negative aspects of carnal man. He symbolizes the desires of the flesh, and such addictions and temptations under his influence will not have a favorable outcome.

Devil Upright

In terms of relationships when the Devil appears in a spread he is warning us about obsession or people that are not good for us. This card is prompting you to look at the situation very carefully. The Devil card warns against destructive consequences as a result of one's actions that are motivated by greed, lust and or power. The Devil is not all a bad omen; he reminds us to change our course of behavior while we can. He is also saying if you have any addictions that you should consciously be aware of how they are damaging you and others around. This card is signaling that you need to gain control over them ASAP. What is interesting about the Devil card in a spread if it is in a favorable position and if marriage or a commitment is in the air; then this is a good omen of a marriage or a commitment. So, in a positive sense the Devil can represent commitment and permanence. Depending where this card falls could mean money matters and a feeling of burden in relation to material aspects of one's life. It indicates the persons desire for physical and material things. This card can also imply the person has feelings of frustration and oppression. When we see this card depending where it is in a spread it can also mean the person has a tendency to collect and hoard both money and objects. This is a card of lust and sexual obsession. It also questions one's security at the expense of their creative or spiritual fulfillment.

The Devil Reversed

When the Devil appears reversed in a reading it also has a duality of meanings. It can mean there is light being shown to us at the end of a long struggle. It can signal that burdens are being lifted or depending on the rest of the cards can indicate true evil. Reversed the Devil talks of abuse of power or authority. This person is so focused on material success that they forget about everything else. It can represent uncontrolled ambition too. Greed, bondage either to a person or situation, emotional black mail and more severe forms of the above are depicted by the Devil in reverse. It is in this position that we are looking at something or someone truly evil depending on the surrounding cards.

XVI
The Tower
Ruler: Mars

Along with Death and The Devil cards; The Tower is a card that causes us to be scared when we see it in a spread. This card is about unexpected upheavals, unexpected shocks and unexpected events that turn our lives upside down; to create new opportunities and make us a stronger and wiser person.

The Tower Upright

The changes that occur when the Tower is in the spread is usually sudden and gives us a jolt. Depending where it falls in a spread it can also represent problems and delays with things like buying a new home or things related to the home front. It represents, tyranny and revolution. The Tower represents the overthrowing of your existing way of life. Whether the source of creating our being upset is material or emotional; this card also encourages you to see the discourse as something to force you into a new and better direction. The Tower can also mean this is a phase and it will pass so a new direction and opportunities can emerge from it.

The Tower represents disruption and confusion. It's a card of major changes and can also mean a sudden violent loss for someone. Depending where it falls in the spread it can appear to mean disruption of a routine that is at the end of its course as well. When we see this card it is saying to us it's time to stop doing the same old tired things. It can portend ruin, disturbances, dramatic upheaval, widespread repercussions of actions and or a change of job and residence at one time. In the end of the towers cycle freedom and enlightenment is brought to the one going through the Tower phase. It means now is the time to re-evaluate things; that this change is necessary and that better will come from this turmoil. It's actually a blessing in disguise depending on the other cards in the spread.

Tower Reversed

There isn't that much difference with the Tower reversed except that the cycle is coming to an end. Reversed the Tower is saying its almost time to start rebuilding. Reversed the Tower can mean negativity. It indicates there is restrictions and some sort of imprisonment whether its physical, emotional or spiritual. Depending where in the spread; the Tower reversed can mean that there are drastic changes that are robbing the person of their freedom of expression. It can also mean bankruptcy or going to jail; imprisonment literally. And more over the reason for the imprisonment cannot be altered at the moment the person will have to do the time for the crime. The reversed Tower can mean sudden changes that one cannot control and lesser meanings of all that this card represents.

The Star
XVII
Ruler: Aquarius

When we see the star it's a bright light to illuminate our ways. It's a welcoming sign. It's a card that is telling us if we look to our personal star blessings will come.

The Star Upright

The Star brings optimism, hope, renewal of faith and unexpected gifts. It is a card of good health. Whether one is considering a new relationship or enterprise this card is a good omen for them. This card speaks of good things. It can mean good times for the person in relation to artistic or educational endeavors, travel, awareness or spiritual development. It is a positive card representing generosity, serenity, fresh hopes and renewal. This card is about when you wish upon a star your wishes come true. Depending on its position in the spread it talks about healing old wounds. It is also a card of spiritual love. This card indicates that the person is broadening their mental and physical horizons. It is also a card of protection. If you were worried that you weren't safe when this card shows up its telling you that you are. The Star is a card of inspiration and the person has the ability to influence others. The person who has this in their spread has vigor and confidence right now.

The Star Reversed

When the Star comes reversed it means we doubt our selves. It warns us that self doubt ruins the possibility of opportunities. It can also mean poor heath or sickness. It also indicates when reversed this person is stubborn. They are either unwilling on incapable to adapt to changing circumstances which prevents them from seeing the opportunities that change may bring. This person lacks trust, in themselves as well as others. Depending where this card falls in a spread it can indicate this person is experiencing obstacles to their happiness. The Star reversed can denote a diminished life. This person has trouble expressing themselves and their mind is rigid. What is interesting is that even reversed this card can bring luck despite the persons cynicism. It teaches us in that case to make lemonade out of lemons.

**XVIII
The Moon
Ruler: Pisces**

This is a card of emotions that run high and feelings of confusion in the form of uncertainty and fear. Just like moonlight it is also a card of illumination as well as unexpected possibilities. It also tells us this person has perception and there are things surrounding them that are not true to the eye.

The Moon Upright

Depending on its position the Moon can mean a clandestine affair; but in the upright position it's a favorable omen for that relationship to be able to emerge into the public eye. If it's not in a good position it can mean that the secret may be exposed. It also represents the unconscious mind and the imagination. This card denotes the person has psychic perception and dreams of spiritual insights. It also means listen to the meanings in your dreams if it pops up in a spread; and to your inner voice for illumination on something that has you are feeling emotionally. The Moon can also imply the person does psychic and spiritual work. It's a card of illusions. When we see the moon in a spread it could be telling us the person is not able to see things clearly and it results in their depression. In this case it also says the person is not in control of their daily living. But even if the going is rough the Moon does however light the way for you to take the right path. Depending where the Moon is in the spread also portends of artistic abilities such as writing or music and that using ones artistic talents can lead to unexpected opportunities. It's also favorable to those in the acting and entertainment industry.

The Moon Reversed

When the moon is reversed it tells of lack of progress because of deep rooted fears and anxieties. It also implies the person lacks nerve in relation to a situation. It warns of lies and deceit which may be the cause of worry for the person. It signals either they are lying or they feel someone is not being straight with them. In general: the reversed Moon is an exaggeration of the upright implications in a reading. Depending where it lies in a spread reversed indicates there is a need for secrecy, there is a deception, illusion, and the person daydreams to escape from reality. It also suggests the person has trouble distinguishing fantasy from reality. Depending where it is in the spread the Moon also talks of insincere people, hidden forces and trickery. It implies the person has trouble telling the truth because they are not capable of it. When it is in reverse the Moon is saying this person is desperate and in need of help; they are in despair.

XIX
The Sun
Ruler: The Sun

Just as we feel happy on a Sunny Warm day so is the blessings of the Sun. It tells of all the good things that we have in our lives and that there is more to come. This is definitely one of the best cards in the Tarot Deck. It is the most welcome of cards portending omens of joy and very happy times.

The Sun Upright

When we see the Sun pop up it can connote holidays, good news concerning children, and even a birth of a much wanted baby. When it pops up in a spread it dispels negativity and promises things will turn out happy. It heralds happy times with family, friends, agreeable companions and relationships. When we see this card we should know that we are going to be content, happy and obtain the success we have been wanting. Depending on where it lays in the spread it can mean material wealth or happiness and good health. The Sun is a card about mental, emotional and spiritual vitality. Besides just happiness; it is a card that implies enlightenment, fulfillment and love. Also depending on where it falls it could mean you are an inventor or have inventions. This card also signals academic success especially in the field of science. It is a card of reward, acclaim, approval abundance of energy and achievement.

The Sun Reversed

When we see the sun reversed its telling us there is trouble in at arrogance and misjudgments are due to an inflated ego.

XX
Judgment
Ruler: Fire and Pluto

This card is one of ultimate justice as in the sentence of Judgment. It is one of Karma being judged by a higher power which sentences our fates. This card finalizes in our lives what we reap is what we will sow

Judgment

The Judgment card tells us that all our hard efforts will finally be rewarded. It says we should take stock and heed of our lives up to this point. When this card appears it is signaling you take into consideration a brand new phase of your life. It implies if one has had bad health that recovery is now in effect and also gives the person a new lease on life. The Judgment card brings with it an opportunity that you must accept; it may come in the form of a decision or project but it should not be ignored because it will change your life. When we see the Judgment card in a spread it means things in our life will start speeding up now. It denotes a rebirth, a time to rejoice, new potential and rewards for the past hard efforts. It is a card of change and improvement. It also implies a satisfactory outcome to a specific matter or period of life. When we see this card it is telling us that we will experience joy in our accomplishments. Depending on where it is in the layout; it tells of awakening. When we see this card it means that it is a good time for career moves. It says we are in a period of mental clarity. It can also mean that an important decision that was pending will change our life for the better.

Judgment Reversed

The first thing we know when we see the Judgment card reversed is there is stagnation around us. There is a delay with concluding a series of actions. Depending where the reversed Judgment card shows up in a spread can imply the person has fear of change and sometimes fears death. In relation to the other cards it can also mean fear of almost everything in this person's life. It also tells us that there is lack of progress in this person's life due to a lack of important decision making on their part. One can also experience temporary loss or separation when Judgment is reversed. Guilt also is implied when the Judgment card is reversed. There is a sense of self reproach with this person and obstinacy. Judgment in reverse warns about self doubt and guilt over past mistakes which blur's one's way forward.

XXI
The World
Ruler: Saturn

This card is a card of confirming that the world is at your command. That all you have to do is stay on a positive course and it's your oyster. But if you choose not to follow the good fortune of your direction the world won't be yours.

The World Upright

The World in a Spread tells us that you are about to get your heart's desire. This includes things like achievement, recognition, success and triumph. The world signals a time of enjoyment. It can take the form of a holiday or travel or time with loved ones. It signals a fulfilling relationship is being offered to you as is spoiling yourself with the material things you have been wanting. The world also signals the end of one cycle to begin another. It is a card that speaks of fulfillment, completion, satisfaction, joy, wholeness and success. This card represents a completed personal cycle, project or series of events or a finished chapter in one's life. The World can also represent a culmination of events. The person has a sense of wholeness.

The World Reversed

When we see the World reversed in a spread it means the delays you are experiencing are challenges you have to overcome in order to succeed. It also means don't give up when you are so close to winning even though the challenges make you want to. It also implies not to lack vision or feel insecure because you are soon to be successful. Reversed this card indicates the person is frustrated. Depending on the spread it indicates delays to completion or that there is an inability to bring things to a successful conclusion. It also implies the person is resistant to change and lacks trust in the process. The reversed World tells of stagnation, lack of will and impatience with the delays and hesitation. It also suggests that the events have not come to a conclusion yet but are nearing the end.

So this is the major arcana and its meanings for the twenty two cards. Of course there are many other variations and explanations to add to these interpretations. As you grow as a reader your interpretation of the cards will be fine tuned for your type of readings.

Chapter 5

The Minor Arcana

We looked at the Major Arcana in the previous chapter; now we come to the Minor Arcana. The Minor Arcana are 56 cards. Like a playing deck of cards it is broken into four suits; each suit having 4 court cards with it. The Major Arcana called the Trump cards deal with life's important issues we face. The Minor Arcana deal with everyday issues and tell us the best way to handle them. Each suit touches on an aspect of our daily lives.

Wands

The first suit we will look at is the Wands. Also called Staff's and Batons. Wands represent fire, the southern direction and summer. The wand cards have to do with primal energy, growth, the will, inspiration, determination, strength, invention, intelligence, creativity and intuition. In our daily lives this card represents our career paths. Wands spiritually mirror what is important to you in your inner being.

Represented by the element of fire wands indicates all the things you do during the course of a day that keeps you busy. Be it at work, at home or the outdoors. Wands are about ideas, growth, ambition and expansion. They also represent our original thoughts and how they are seeds through which life springs. If there are many wands in a reading it indicates the conditions in which the querent finds themselves in based first in thought; and then as ideas being in the first stages of development.

The fire signs are related to the wands; Aries, Leo and Sagittarius. The South is the direction for the wands. The physical characteristics of people in relation to this suit are: fair skinned with red to blond to light brown hair and blue to green or light eyes. Wands are related to Spring and weeks in terms of time. So if you see the 4 of wands it may mean 4 weeks.

Ace Of Wands

Divinatory Meaning:

Upright:

The essence of fire; this card denotes a new job, career or enterprise is in the making for the querent. This card signals creativity, inventiveness, ambition and enthusiasm. It is a card that in principle symbolizes the beginning of something. It can be a birth, an idea, the starting point of a enterprise. Ace of Wands can mean the aggressive pursuit of new ventures. The foundation created for future successes, the person uses their intuition well, fertility and conception is possible. It is also a card of manhood and artistic innovation.

Reversed:

Setbacks in a new endeavor. Lack of determination or selfishness may hamper a projects completion. A high indication of treachery prevalent. Disagreement, imminent danger as is loss of purity. Depending on where it falls in the spread it can indicate a false start, a cancellation of a plan, trip or business venture. The reversed Ace of Wands can also signal bareness, sterility, impotence, avarice and greed. Reversed it signals an over confidence that ends in tears. If the querent is a woman it can indicate that she has trouble with men. Reversed it can also mean clouded joy or fall, decadence, ruin and perdition to perish.

**II of Wands
Dominion**

Upright:

The number two represents a union, the joining together of often opposing forces, spoke. The two thus represents a "concretization" of the energy represented in the ace. The Ace of Wands signified the fiery energy of inspiration. The Two of Wands represents the beginning of clarity, the formulation of the spark of inspiration into an idea which can be carried out.

The Two of Wands represents a mature person who may provide you with assistance to obtain your desires. The person is hoping that something good is about to happen and wants to see it materialize. An offer is about to be presented. If you don't feel right about it or it isn't enough, don't sell yourself short or settle for less. There is something better on the horizon.

In practical terms this card indicates success that has been achieved through hard work. The querent has strength of character and is making sure that their ideas come to fruition. They use their power and wisdom responsibly as it was gained through experience. This card indicates wealth that is obtained legally and there are job related perks for this person. The Two of Wands means the person is taking control of their territory with action. They are making something their own. It represents the querent or the person in question making a statement of ownership.

Reversed:

Reversed this card is telling the querent that naked ambitions knows no bounds. Domination by others. A good beginning may turn against you. You are in for a surprise of some kind.

Conceit, aloofness, losing strength, imprudence, weak defenses, losing momentum after a good start, disappointment, frustration, impatience, pride, short sighted goals, being blocked, disconnected, breakdown of negotiations, self serving, sadness, loss of faith, second thoughts, empty success, things go sour, dominated by others, fear and weakness in the face of conflict, complacency are all associated with the reverse of the Two of Wands. Reversed it also implies that riches and fortunes are obtained illegally, dishonestly or by deception. When this card is in reverse it indicates the person in question has lost faith in both their own rationale and self. They are in attainment of worthless ambition.

III of Wands

Upright:

The number Three represents the initial fulfillment of the union of opposites symbolized in the number two.

When we see the III of wands in a spread we know that our actions are increased to succeed.

The Three of Wands shows a person standing on a hill gazing far out into the distance. It indicates you in a position of strength as you control what happens around you. This is a card of vision and foresight - looking for greater possibilities. This card asks you to be a visionary - to dream beyond current limitations. The Three of Wands tells you that now is the time to accept your vision and be confident that you will achieve it. You are being encouraged to move fearlessly into new areas. Dreams turn into reality through the circumstances. You are in the right place at the right time lending to your success. Successful ventures are launched and there is inspiration of original ideas. Your success lies in the courage of your convictions. Your plans and ventures are moving ahead.

Reversed:

In its reversed position, the Three of Wands may indicate a lack of cooperation, wasted efforts, delays, or bad luck. It implies obstacles from outside in commercial or communication ventures. The querent may feel a creative block, and find that their goals are hard to reach. Their problem may involve over-confidence, pride, or arrogance on their part. They need to be open to receiving help and input from others, but know at the same time that opposition may come from a person who exploits other people for material gain. There is the possibility of betrayal of an enterprise by a person who had the power to aid it. The querent may have set their expectations too high. Possibly they may need to reset their goals so that they are more realistic. The querent or one close to them must deal with difficulties in the exchange of goods or ideas as well with matters of trust. This card suggests failure to put one's plans into actions. The goals you strive for are not attainable right now. There is lack of communication between what you dream and what is reality. You have trouble distinguishing between the two. Great plans that do not come into fruition. This person retreats from reality into fantasy.

IV Of Wands

Upright:

The Four of Wands if one of the most positive cards in the Tarot deck and indicates general good fortune, satisfaction, and fulfillment. The four indicates a sense of harmony and balance as well as completion, and thus symbolizes a time of peace and joy in life that come as the result of often difficult and challenging effort. If you encounter this card in a reading, there is cause for celebration!

When we see this card upright it indicates celebration and ceremony upon completion. Optimism and joy. Relaxation. It indicates that now is a good time to move in new directions. Something is completed or something initiated. Contented home life. Prosperity. Harvest. A successful conclusion. Personal achievement, material well being. This is a card of the home. Improvements to property or imminent move. Working with people.

Celebration of recent good fortune; marriage or good solid business relationship; the successful completion of the initial stage of a project; cooperation, heading in the same direction, of the same mind; the coming together of ideas; satisfaction with current situation. When we see this card in our spread it means that there is a successful completion to all the hard work we put in and we can see the fruits of our labor. This card indicates marriage or a new romance. The IV of Wands is card of the professional man; he is an innovator and can be a renown designer. The establishment of culture, Refinement, charm, attractiveness and splendor. The Four of Wands also indicates contentment through the association of another person in a romantic setting.

Reversed:

When the Four of Wands appears reversed it means there is a lack of commitment; shaky relationship; difference of opinion and a change in goals in a partnership; failure in initial stage of project; dissatisfaction and loss of tranquility; disorder; too many ideas to act upon.

It can however also signal that there is happiness but it is in an unconventional and unorthodox way. It also implies that this person guides their life by superfluous and artificial constraints and rules. Traditions has made this person an innate snob, who feels their pomp and ceremony rain supreme over others. It can also signal a rest period before successful completion of something.

V of Wands

Upright:
Five people of different colors fight each other. This card lets you know there is a major competition going on Competition. What the 5 of Wands is saying to you is you need

to experience what competition really means and requires. Respect your opponent, but stand up for your point of view. Refuse to be a victim. Fight the tendency towards frustration, anger, hate and prejudice.

This card is representative of a group of people who are committed to an end, but they cannot fully agree on how to effectuate this goal, as each has his/her individual agenda as to how to bring this to fruition. The struggle represented in the Five of Wands does not necessarily imply the end of the satisfaction and joy symbolized in the Four of Wands. Rather, this card represents the challenges presented to any vision or creative effort by the world or by one's competitors. The joys of a wedding are often followed by domestic struggle to define the boundaries of the relationship and to begin to understand one another in greater depth. The initial success of a creative venture or business is often followed by challenges from rivals who sense success and want to partake of it themselves, perhaps even at your expense.

When we see this card in a spread it warns of problems and upheavals that cannot be avoided. It can even be in the form of minor irritations that test us. It indicates one has to have great mental agility and use their own inner mental resources to win the situation. In this case the only way success is won is through hard persistence. One has to be a relentless worker when this card appears. This card depicts combat and strife, but the rivalry conveyed is not necessarily based on anger.

It can represent heated arguments and even physical violence if next to a card of conflict, such as the Three of Swords, Five of Swords, or Seven of Swords. Usually however, when found next to more neutral cards, the Five of Wands represents the competition necessary to promote business or an idea.

Reversed:

This card is like a sigh of relief after conflict and struggle when we see it in reverse. Now the client can afford to relax his efforts a bit and reap the benefits of his previous promotional efforts. In a more personal sense, he has worked through his anger and hostility and feels more secure in his interpersonal relationships. He doesn't feel he has to constantly prove himself anymore. The Reversed V of Wands indicates harmony in affairs. Love of exercise and games. Generosity. New business opportunity. Victory after obstacles are overcome. Expect to have to overcome trickery and deceit to get what you want.

Don't relax all the way when this card shows in a spread reversed because it can also mean trickery, hurt, fraud, defeat and ruin mostly of someone else that you were fighting. It can also mean litigation and legal tiffs that can be avoided. Depending what cards surround the V of Wands it also implies competition that is unnecessary and spiteful conversations.

V of Wands

Upright:

The VI of Wands indicates triumph/victory in your situation. You'll be able to progress in the development of all that's in your best interests. Progress may be in the form of good news which you receive, permitting you to proceed with your desires. This card indicates you want to get on with things in your life. You are going to start a new project, way of life, or life style. Conditions of renewal are approaching, and when that happens, the time will be right and things will come together.

The VI of Wands, like the Four, represents an achievement or success in the pursuit of a creative venture. However, the VI of Wands contains a more public element of recognition by others in one's community for the fulfillment of a creative effort on one's behalf. This card indicates a struggle has been overcome, the goal has been reached, and it is publicly acknowledged and celebrated. Victory, success, an out-of-town visitor, a trip or tour all can be a message that this card brings depending on the spread. Combined with the Ace of Wands it can mean a book-signing tour or international world recognition. If it appears with the VIII of Pentacles it signals a successful sales representative. The VI of Wands, like the Four, represents an achievement or success in the pursuit of a creative venture. A struggle has been overcome, the goal has been reached, and it is publicly acknowledged and celebrated.

When we see this card it denotes the arrival of good and fantastic news. If you are taking a trip it will prove successful. This is a card of victory. Success and acclaim for all your hard work is signaled when we see this card. There is hope and satisfaction due to what you accomplished. This card means you can overcome obstacles with tact and diplomacy rather than by the use of force.

Reversed:

When this card appears reversed it means one's rewards are delayed. Bad news in wake of victory. Watch out for a successful enemy. When V1 of Wands appears reversed its telling us that there is indecision involving in our situation. It also denotes that the enemy is up to no good and engaging in surreptitious activities. It suggest that the person is fearful about an outcome in a situation. Reversed it implies delayed news and even possibly bad news.

VII of Wands

Upright:

The VII of Wands, like the Five, again presents a struggle after the initial experience of satisfaction and fulfillment. In this case, the character in the card stands at the top of a hill and is challenged from below by opponents seeking to achieve the success and status of the victor. It signals that the creative, successful individual must continually struggle to maintain his or her position at the "top." If your vision and creative effort is fulfilled to the point where there is public acclaim or acceptance of your success then you must expect competition and challenge. It is a point of fact because others may also desire the same things as you.

Now the Sevens are all about attaining higher wisdom- through a process of testing, internal examination, and choice. You will find a challenge in each of these cards; and you will need to use different techniques to meet and overcome that challenge. Remember, each card in the Tarot talks about, among other things, a process. Taken together, these processes describe the ways in which we conduct our lives, constructively and destructively.

The VII of Wands is all about struggle. It's about standing up for who we are and what we are. In a sense, this is one of the "boundary" cards, because, when you see it, you know that things have reached a point beyond which you do not want to go. Negotiation is over, when this card appears. In order to maintain your personal integrity, you are going to have to be firm. If you're lucky, you can just be firm quietly, and those around you will respect your stance. If not, though, you might have to "fight" for what you believe, want or need. This can take several forms, of course, from a firm statement to an all out "war." What is at stake is your own self-image. We all have a line which we will not let others step past, and this card is telling the reader is it.

On the negative side, this card can manifest in one of two ways. It can indicate an unwillingness to stand up for yourself. The eternal martyr can be found here. But it can also indicate bickering. At its worst, it is one of the most confrontational cards in the deck-because the energy that drives it is pure unadulterated childish ego. Fighting just to fight. It's the person who wakes up angry and gets worse as the day progresses.

If you're doing a relationship spread, you don't want to see this card with the Three of Swords. I can almost guarantee you that this combination indicates discord of the worst kind. See, the Three of Swords can indicate expressing thoughts which are based on a misunderstanding. And it can indicate quarreling. This card describes a situation in which you fail to defend your position due to a lack of willpower. You are feeling outnumbered, victimized and helpless. The good news is that you are able to defend yourself against the onslaught. It is a card of successful advancement. When we see this card it means we have an opportunity that requires great skill, and you need to use your courage and determination to win. This card indicates strength of nerve, great fortitude and courage in face of a hardship. Success will be gained through sustained effort. This is a card of defense. It warns though, that the offense is strong and a powerful contender.

Reversed:
Threat will pass you by. Don't let others take advantage of you. Patience in the face of threats. The querent may be threatened. When the VII of Wands appears in reverse it indicates indecision and retreat. If one does not act decisively the situation causing the challenge will be lost. In reverse this card indicates loss through hesitation and giving up when the end is in sight. Depending on the surrounding cards it can mean turning away from opportunities due to fear of responsibilities.

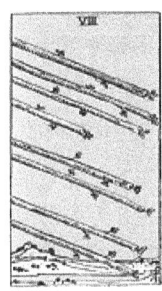

VIII of Wands

Upright:
The Eight of Wands denotes speed and rapid advancement of the querent's situation in general. This haste could result in wrong decisions being made. It will be important to have all your resources available to be used in your best interests. This card indicates that you want to speed things up, settle a matter of concern, or branch out on your own. You're approaching your goal, but your affairs will not be completely set, decided, or determined. The VIII of Wands represents a very focused kind of motion. The eights are all about structure. And the wands, being fire, are the most volatile kind of energy. So the structure doesn't produce something static in this case. Instead, it creates a narrow channel through which the energy rushes.

The VIII of Wands indicates quick change and action. It is a card of understand and harmony. Good news and communication. This card indicates the time is right for facilitating success. Swift and speedy end to delays. It is a card of fast news or correspondence which is favorable. It can also indicate travel or important trip. In general it is a hopeful card.

Health issues: When we see this card it tells us health wise about adrenal depletion; breathlessness; fertility; ribs; arteries; male sexual (premature ejaculation/too fertile)

Reversed:

Jealousy is in the air when we see the VIII of Wands reversed. A message you have been waiting to hear has not yet shown up. Do not become too bold or too courageous. Business slows down and your love life ends up at a standstill. When it appears reversed it indicates disputes and disagreements. It indicates a great effort and driving force that was wasted because the person ran out of steam. Delays in news. It can mean depending on the surrounding cards silly spontaneous actions. A trip is cancelled. This card indicates you will jump into the water head first without testing it first when reversed.

IX of Wands

When we encounter the IX of Wands we are often in the midst of a challenge that appeared just when we thought all was won. This challenge comes at the moment before our final accomplishment of a creative task or goal. The card indicates that we have the inner resources necessary to overcome any difficulty we encounter, even though it may seem impossible at the time. How often do we give up just before we finally achieve success? This card is a sign of hope and encouragement; that if we stand firm and strong against challenge, we will achieve our goal. The challenges before us are only the last bit of darkness before the break of wonderful dawn.

The number nine is the number of completion. It is the final stage of all the numbers that have come before it. In this number we also see tiny little seeds of new beginnings being planted to take root. The Nine of Wands represents a man who has been knocked down and around, beaten, yet he has overcome all that he has gone through. He has fought the battle and won. He appears drained and weary as he leans on his wand, but is ready to go to battle again. He stands up for what he believes in and holds firm in those beliefs. He is secure in who he is. This card represents being prepared. Eventual victory is won with more fighting. Defense of oneself. This card signals strong opposition of those who do you wrong. The IX of Wands indicates strength. You will be opposed by secret enemies and your interests will be questioned. Unexpected difficulties with all situations. It will be necessary then, to have support available to help you overcome these obstacles. This card indicates you want your efforts to bear fruit, you wish to socialize, circulate and be out with others, and your health (or that of another) will improve. If you don't succeed at first, try again. Also, expect good news concerning business, love, or finances. One last test or challenge remains. You feel as if you've come to the end of your fighting powers, but you have skill and determination in reserve. You're actually in a position of strength.

Although you'll need to draw on all your courage and abilities, you prevail. Be patient. Keep your own counsel. Once the last obstacle is overcome, you're home free. You are in order and if you utilize your discipline you will be in an unassailable position. Any opposition you face will be defeated. You have courage in the face of attack and your stability cannot be removed.

Health issues This card signals head injury; shoulder; knee; ankle; jaw (TMJ); bladder meridian. However if the other cards are favorable surrounding it; it can mean good health.

Reversed:

The IX of Wands reversed suggests that you may be hesitant to make a long-term commitment. You might be feeling as if life is all work and no play. This cad indicates you are feeling overcome by responsibilities or a lack of support from those around you. As such, you are hesitant to make any commitments in fear that the responsibilities will become all too much. Be careful also of dwelling on past frustrations and grievances. Just try to let go.

You may also be more inclined to be a little 'on edge' and on the defensive when we see this card in a spread. The boundaries you have set around yourself are now becoming your cage, locking you into your old habits and behaviors. Be careful not to assume things or make hasty judgments. Lighten up a little and return to the VIII of Wands where you take life as it comes in all its various forms. Go with the flow and release yourself of the pressures you are feeling.

A holiday or a break might do you some good where you can re-energize and rejuvenate yourself. When this card appears in reverse it talks of rigidity and not being able to give and take. If you have undertaken any projects they will fail now because they are impractical in nature. Depending on the spread it can indicate disarray and delays. Where if falls in the spread can indicate poor health or illness. This card is signaling that a position that once was secure is no longer. Lastly this person has personality flaws that get in their way.

X of Wands

Meaning

This card, like all others in the Tarot deck, has both positive and negative aspects to consider. In one sense, he is reaping a bountiful reward for hard work in his harvest. In this case it represents our own success after a long and perhaps difficult struggle. This card can also mean being oppressed by outside sources, overworked, over tired or over stimulated. It indicates that you Have more on your plate (or back) than you can possibly handle. This card talks about being overwhelmed at its worst. Life and everything in it becomes a burden, and each little task just adds weight. People who are moving to new homes in a month's time get this a lot; and you can see why. This card implies the person is carrying of a weighty load. Their heart is tried by pain. It can mean ruin of all plans and projects; complete disruption and failure. But, if you are experiencing any of the problems they may soon be solved. It is a card of oppression.

You need to stop working so hard. If you cannot stop, then conserve your energy and pace yourself. When you are over-committed everything becomes a strain. There will be a delay making decisions if exhaustion prevents good judgment. This card signals burdens, responsibilities, resentfulness.

Perseverance will be met with success, though one's health may suffer. Heavy duties, difficult tasks are all implied when this card is in a spread. You will be successful even though in terms of health and anxiety, the price may be high.

Perhaps some obligations have to go. The overload is not through choice or planning, but just "happened" as a part of life. This is a person who "bends over backwards", often in a relationship, in order to try and make it work. The other person meanwhile is not even aware how much the they are trying to carry the relationship.

On the other hand this persons conduct is honorable. Great fortune has become a burden due to its demanding nature and the time it involves. Due to the economy a business may have to be downsized. A successful past time can no longer be administered by the person who created it. This person has no social life due to the demands of a project and the overtime they put in.

Health issues - tension (neck and shoulder); headaches; vision; overwork.

Reversed:

When the X of Wands is reversed it indicates that strength and energy a person applies is for selfish ends. Desire to ruin happiness of others. If a lawsuit is pending there may be loss. When this card appears reversed it is warning of a jealousy that is going to great lengths to spoil the persons pleasures and affairs. It can also denote treachery. This person has trouble delegating responsibilities to others resulting in unnecessary stress for them. Depending on the spread in reverse this card means someone is using lies and deceit to upset others.

Court Cards

Page of Wands

Meaning Upright

Physical description – yellow to red hair, blue eyes. A young person, or a likeable stranger.

Personality traits - helpful, mild mannered, friendly, polite, adaptable, hard working, enthusiastic, impulsive, may be hyperactive with little staying power, easily bored.

Meaning:

The Page of the Wands is the loyal envoy and emissary of the royal family. He is a trusted friend who is devoted to your interests. His intentions will be honorable. You need not fear trusting what he has to say on the behalf of another person. This card indicates the querent wants things to change (this could be concerning a loved one). It also signals the person needs to break free of oppression or stagnation in business or find a solution to problems. Change is in the air, and a new approach is at hand. This could come through a friend who will help you to 'see the light' or attain a new perspective.

The Page of Wands can be used to identify a young person with a rather melancholy outlook. Alternately, some readers interpret this card to mean a near relative or a close friend of the querent. It also indicates a messenger, messages, telephone calls, and official communications. Receiving communication so a decision can be made. Someone is trying to tell you something.

When the Page of Wands represents a new event, the event may concern work or business. Maybe a new work project is available. In a reading regarding spiritual issues, the Page of Wands could indicate a spiritual aspect to a practical matter. For instance, a trip the querent is about to undertake for business reasons may bring a new spiritual meaning to the person's life in an unexpected manner. The Page of Wands could also indicate a new beginning of a practical, business or career nature, such as a new job, a new development in the person's career field.

Some readers also interpret the Page of Wands as a possible new residence. When we see this card it tells us the person is trustworthy and a reliable young person. This person desires to bring happiness, excitement and light to those around. When we see this card in the spread we know the person is faithful as a messenger of good news and witty gossip. They are a dedicated person of service to superiors.

Page of Wands Reversed

The Page of Wands reversed depicts a person who is immature with a self-image problem. It could be someone who is mean-spirited and aggressive, or someone who is helpless and always a "victim." This is someone who never has anything good to say, is always pessimistic, and always brings everyone down. This person undercuts your enthusiasm and your self-confidence. This person hasn't earned much admiration or respect, but surely expects it anyway. This is a superficial, lazy and arrogant person; one who is unwilling to make an effort, and is uncooperative and impatient.

When the card appears reversed the honest qualities the person has changes to petulance. You may have thought this person was trustworthy but all the time they are dishonest. This person cannot keep a confidence. You cannot trust them. They lie and spread gossip. In reverse it can also mean a delay or change of residence.

Knight of Wands

Meaning Upright:

Physical Description - yellow, red hair, blue eyes, young, strong, person. Robust, ruddy complexion.

Personality Traits - eager to help, trustable. Takes risks, puts energy into self-growth, future prospects and new directions. Energetic warrior. Hasty personality. Quick to love or hate.

The Knight of Wands is a really sparkly guy. The fiery element of the wands gives him an enthusiastic and innovating approach, a great help to get things started. Knights, like all court cards, do not necessarily reflect one gender. The knight can be male or female.

In women, he can represent the animus, or inner assertive side, of their character. The Knight of Wands represents mental intuition, a sudden and impetuous nature, a generous friend or lover. He or she is hasty in everything.

This card indicates there may be a journey or change in residence. A male friend or relative is willing to help the querent. The Knight of the Wand indicates the departure of something or someone. A journey could be indicted as well as the advancement of your position in the situation being addressed. Where the Page of Wands represents the immature beginnings of a new idea or creative adventure that exists only as a "castle in the sky"; the Knight of Wands represents the active pursuit of that adventure. Since the suit of Wands is analogous to the alchemical element of fire, this knight is representative of the hot passion of inspiration in search of fulfillment. Unlike the Page of Wands who simply dreams his dream; the Knight actively pursues his vision with an abandon that is characteristic of the impulsive astrological sign of Aries. This is a person who loves action. He is well liked and ambitious but has an unpredictable nature. His temperament is engaging and although he moves quickly his actions make sense later on in hindsight.

Reversed

The Knight of Wands reversed indicates delays and frustration, getting nowhere and feeling anger at obstacles. It can represent the feeling of being denied what you want to have. This card, in the reversed position, represents a loss of personal power or the negative use of power. It can indicate that you are trying to camouflage or compensate for your inability to control this situation. Accompanying emotions in relation to the reversed Knight of Wands would involve a loss of self-esteem and pessimism. He can be so over enthusiastic it clashes with the personalities of those around him. When reversed this person likes discord, arguments, strife and trouble just for the sake of it. He will actively seek those destructive elements and cause them if they aren't already in motion. In reverse this card can also mean delays with a trip.

Queen of Wands

Meaning

Physical Description - yellow, red hair, blue eyed woman. She runs a business or holds a responsible position.

Personality traits - intelligent, dignified, prosperous woman, self-confidence, love of happiness. Offers help that you can trust. She offers inspiration. Fiery temperament. Lively, active, warm natured. Practical organizer of others. A lover of nature.

The Queen of Wands expresses a creative energy. In decks where wands are fire, she has a fiery, passionate personality with a quick temper. Her style of mothering is to 'flash' her temper, yell, then get over it and hug -- all within one hour! She's self-confident and happy. You have recently met (or will meet) someone you could have a relationship with and are wondering if you should, or if you will. True guidance proves itself, in that it brings with it the action, or ability to carry it out. If you are in a quandary, remember that decisions usually make themselves when the time comes.

The Queen of Wands loves the country and prefers to live there. She can be a good business woman however. She is both fair and capable in her dealings with others. She is fertile in body and mind and makes a good homemaker as well. She does well in social settings and is charming. The Queen of Wands can be very protective to those in her circle. This card can also indicate success in a project.

Reversed

This card describes a situation in which someone is behaving in a manipulative, pushy or selfish way. Your or someone close seems to be in a chronically bad mood, is angry, resentful and jealous. You may find yourself being attacked or bullied, or behaving yourself this way. Perceptions are skewed and information is being twisted into lies. Someone is demanding, controlling, petty and narrow-minded.

When this card is reversed this person is dominating and or bitter.

She's the overbearing matriarchal type. The Queen of Wands reversed is cruel, has a very dry sense of humor, is paranoid in the sense that she always thinks people are out to get her even when they have no malice towards her what so ever.

King of Wands

Physical description - yellow, red hair, blue eyed older man. Brown hair. Athletic, strong, healthy.

Personality traits - creative, self-expressive, domineering, showy, theatrical, likes to gamble. Has power and influence. They know when to take action, and create harmonious human relationships. This person has a good sense of humor. Also they are honorable in old fashioned sense. Much travelled, Just, kind, generous. Excellent adviser. Sexually passionate.

Meaning:

The King of Wands is a passionate guy who will sweep you off your feet with wine and roses. He knows how to romance women. The problem is, he may not hold on to them once he has them. He's always looking for the bigger, better deal. He's creative, passionate and jealous. The King of Wands it the political activist, an artist, or a race car driver. He is a "born-leader" card.

This card represents energy, excitement and confidence. A King of Wands type person is someone people naturally flock to and follow. The King of Wands is able to get things done. Curiously, the King of Wands often does this by getting other people to do the work for him! One danger of the King is that he can be distracted . Furthermore, he's so accustomed to attention that he tends to take people for granted. In this case, the King is reversed. This card can often suggests a blockage or distortion of the card's message. The King of Wands represents the epitome of the qualities we associate with the element of fire. He is strength, leadership, creativity, vision, and the motivation to bring that creative vision into reality.

The King of Wands is the insignia of power and authority. Depending on all cards, the application of this symbolism will change. Power and authority assist or oppose your interests. The assistance may come from another person or be in the form of knowledge.

You want to make contact with someone and/or to be successful in a new business venture. Your action, decision or opinion will be the deciding factor. The negative aspect of the King of Wands stems from his drive and energy which can be interpreted by others as pushiness, arrogance, and an insolent sense of grandeur.

This figure represents a man who is often successful in business life. Romantically, the King of Wands plays two roles.

As a partner or potential lover, he is attractive, generous and uplifting company. His volatile vitality is very seductive, and he enjoys the intensity of intimacy. His love of freedom may manifest in a lifelong enjoyment of the countryside, indeed, wide open spaces are important to him in every way, intellectually, spiritually, and emotionally. The King of Wands can also denote the male lover in a clandestine or illicit affair. The Lovers, reversed, would confirm this meaning, or the Three of Swords could symbolize a love triangle.

He is for the most part charming, responsible, can be loyal, entertaining, witty, honest conscientious and generous. He loves his home and family life. He is passionate and virile. The King of Wands looks for support and encouragement. If he is pushed or provoked he will act without hesitation even though it may be hard for him because he can see both sides of an argument.

Health issues associated with this card: hand problems; headache; control freak; hip; stroke; wheel chair.

Reversed

This personality type can make rash, hasty, and impulsive decisions. The reversed King of Wands signals the person can be dominating, pushy, and overbearing at times. This is rarely done with malice or an intention to make someone else submissive. It is just a strong tendency that sometimes takes control. The King of Wands type usually doesn't even realize when he or she crosses the line between being assertive and aggressive.

When reversed, the King of Wands typifies the most selfish, ruthless qualities of fire. He can denote a manipulative business contact who will use you as long as it serves his purpose. He may be a rival, competitor or unscrupulous opponent. In love, he represents a delightful flirtation that could wreak emotional havoc. He is only suitable for limited liaisons, holiday romances or delicious, but brief, encounters. His flames are bright and warm but soon die down. When this happens he seeks enduring sources of warmth elsewhere. He has the inability to see others point of view nor even appreciate it when reversed. Reversed, his views are even more rigid if the views are not coming from a moral perspective like his own. He has no tolerance, is bigoted, narrow minded with deep prejudices. This person has a ruthless streak and does not care in the least about others feelings when this card is in reversed.

Chapter 6
Cups

Cups in the Tarot deck are likened to the Hearts in a regular playing deck. Cups represent water, the west and autumn. They have to do with love, the emotions, feelings, decisions, finishing stages in one's life, your sensitivity and your family life. The Cups Suit deal with the emotional level of consciousness. Cups mirror your spontaneous responses and your habitual reactions to situations. Cups have an affinity with religious groups or institutions.

The people represented by the Suit of Cups are generally fair, plump people who are emotional, artistic, humane and creative. They are said to correspond to the water signs in the zodiac (Pisces, Cancer, Scorpio) and water as a symbol of the subconscious mind and reason. Cups are associated with anything emotional, from marriage to personal possessions and concerns. This also covers anything relating to partnerships, whether in a work or personal context. Our relationships with others are covered by the Suit of Cups. It is a suit of love and happiness, and the feelings suggested by the suit runs deep. Should a reading be predominantly "cups", then you can be sure that the Querent is seeking solutions to what are primarily emotional conflicts, love matters and emotions.

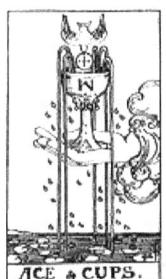

Ace of Cups

Meaning

The Ace of Cups represents the home and general environment. There will be joy in your life with the fulfillment of all your ambitions and desires. Much happiness will be found in your contentment. This card portends you are searching for clarity, or for the truth in a situation where your heart says one thing and your intellect another. Or, it can mean you hope an idea will become a reality. Your ideas will meet with success. There is a chance for a marriage either with love or in business partnership and possible new contract.

Positive air is flowing and it is time to forgive and make up. This is a peaceful time in your life so use it and make this peace with friends or yourself. It is time of fertility, a time for child bearing. Perhaps an adoption should be considered. The Ace of Cups depicts the emergence of spirituality and the awakening of a new awareness of spiritual life. Bliss, open yourself to supreme happiness. The Ace of Cups signals an emotional upsurge, power of imagination, budding sexuality, engaging another, spiritual love or psychic ability, art, first love, closeness, lover, friendship, renewal, water of life, relationship, inspiration, awakening, nurture, abundance, happiness, peace, nourishment, protection, vulnerability, tenderness, fulfilling, good will, fertility, sensitivity, production, higher call. It also talks about the person in relation to compassion, receptivity, devotion, romance, marriage, loving union, reaping the fruits of what you have sown, openness, spiritual vision, the Grail, redemption, regeneration, satisfaction, female principle, imagination, close attachment, intimacy, rebirth, recycle, regrowth, changing, open channel, sentiment, sympathy, empathy, anticipation, longing, being filled, depths, offering, hope, recreation, chalice as womb of life, pleasure, beauty, sensuality, promise. Intuition, purity, calm, unconditional love, primordial, productiveness, excitement, premonition, emotional release, love at first sight, happy home, goodness overflowing, light in the dark, contentment.

It is a card of close relationships, the family, lovers, rivals, premonitions, fears, memories, nostalgia, and most of all water is our unconscious. A huge cup is being offered to you in this card, and you are being invited to reach out to grasp it and drink from it.

What this cup is representing is a symbol of emotional fulfillment, not just on the emotional level, but on the spiritual level as well. Whether you are going to reach out now and partake of this offering is going to depend obviously upon how thirsty you are, upon how much you are in need of being refreshed.

Abundance of love. Joy, celebration. Love with wisdom. Fertility. Marriage, declaration of love, new love, inspired creativity and artistic excellence are all in association with this card. This card signals a love affair. It indicates a Marriage or birth. A blessing from out of the blue. Someone cares for you. A gift, especially of love. A gift of a ring. The Beginning of all good things, whether it be love, joy, beauty or health, a new spiritual understanding. Merriment and celebration of some sort. It is a card of faithfulness and all the positives of the unconscious mind.

Medically this suit refers to the Urinary (kidney and bladder problems) and Reproductive Systems. Water comes to us in the form of blood, tears, urine, perspiration, saliva, and sexual juices. A lack of water can bring about a dried up feeling (stiffness both emotional and physical), lack of moisture in the body, non-flowing with life, difficulty with dealing with emotions and with others who are emotional.

Reversed

Upright, this card represents the feeling of when we are about to burst with all our overflowing emotions, whether it be with complete laughter or tears. Sometimes you get so excited you could bounce around the house screaming out in ecstasy. Or sometimes the pain surrounding you is so great that all you can do is burst into tears. The reversed Ace of Cups is therefore the opposite to this feeling of joyous emotions, and can mean one of many things.

Firstly, the card may call on you to curb your emotions somewhat for your greater benefit. For example, ending a relationship may spur you on to wanting to cry and cry for days on end. But what the Ace of Cups reversed tells us is that in order to heal, we really need to push back the tears and fight on in order to retain a balance. Alternatively, the Ace of Cups could suggest that you have repressed your feelings too long and it is now the time to release them. You may have kept your excitement quiet about the prospect of a new job, in fear of it failing, but now is the time to let those emotions run free. Or, you may have bottled up so many emotional thoughts that you have become almost void of feeling true emotions.

False heart, inconsistency, barren, poor choice of partner, loss of love, being rejected or betrayed, broken heart, divorce, loneliness, separation, sadness, thinking only of one's self, toying with emotions, bruised emotionally, loss of hope, fatigue, unstable emotions, stuck in an emotional rut, in love with love, puppy love, gullible, unrequited love are all the signals of this card reversed. This person is hesitant to accept things of the heart. There is someone with an egotistical false heart. When this card is reversed it is symbolizing the worst; a time of emptiness, whether, physically, emotionally or a combination. It means the person is failing at love, is stagnated, and possibly lost faith in things they believed in.

II of Cups

Meaning Upright

The II of Cups indicates partnership, engagement or friendships. The card is indicative of marriage, romance, passions and emotions. A partnership may be indicated. You will experience love and harmony with your sisters or brothers even if you've had a falling out in the past. The II of Cups shows the beauty and power that is created when two come together. This is the card that lovers want to see, and, in fact, the II of Cups is the Minor Arcana equivalent of the Lovers in many ways.

New relationship, awareness, trust, perceptions, harmony, empathy, marriage, engagement, romance, passion, sharing, contract, pledges and promises, reconciliation, working toward common goals, moving toward permanence, agreement, happiness, social union, faithfulness, mutual care, understanding another, union, cooperation, courtship, platonic love, constancy within change, freedom are all signals of this card depending on the spread. Consummation, proposal, intimacy, reciprocity, yin/yang, polarity, union of opposites, confidence in another, joy and contentment, kindred spirits, equality, attraction, sacred union, sacred marriage, harmony, integrity, equilibrium, free flowing, cooperation, working together, cementing a friendship, bringing opposites together, making peace, forgive and forget, attraction, being drawn in, concord. Cementing relationships. Commitment are all associated with the II of Cups. It signals a union, a partnership or an engagement and Love and understanding between two people.

Harmony (opposites attract). Co-operation. Friendship, ending of rivalry. When we see this card we know a new friendship, romance or partnership is going to begin with the chance for love and affection if this card is in the spread in a favorable position. It shows that the person has an emotional affinity, sympathy and or joyous harmony with another. This card can also represent the reconciliation of opposites now in mutual trust. It can also signify the resolution of differences between people.

Two's generally suggest some type of beginning or initial exercise involving the aspects of the suit. Cups suggest intuitive and emotional aspects (okay, including romance). At a simple level, this card could suggest a possible new friendship or a renewed relationship.

Reversed

When we see the II of Cups reversed its telling us that something is out of balance, there is a troubled relationship, divorce, misunderstanding, lack of trust, inappropriate or unreasonable expectations, break up, separation, false friend, opposition, unrequited love, discord, incompatibility, holding back, isolation, repressed anger, quarrels, emotional pain, betrayed confidence, disillusionment, overindulging in sensuality, infatuation. Depending where it falls in a spread can indicate a loss of balance, violent passion, a misunderstanding with someone the querent values highly.

Since this card is reversed, it also suggests some type of inhibition or distortion regarding the basic message -- perhaps a reluctance to expose your feelings. When this card is reversed it signals the possibility of separation, dissent, divorce, deceit or unfaithfulness in a personal close relationship. The love one feels for another is not mutual or returned. It can also represent quarrels between two close people.

III of Cups

Meaning Upright

The III of Cups is a card of celebration and accomplishment. The three young maidens dance in a circle with their golden goblets upraised in a toast of joy. The ground is covered with fruit and there is a general sense of abundance and happiness. The III of Cups indicates the end or conclusion of any problems in the past. A compromise will be found which will serve all the interests of those involved in a struggle. There will be time to relax after the compromise is implemented.

The III of Cups tells us that since we will be unable to control external conditions, you will realize that we must change internally, and will want to revise our attitude and the way we react or deal with what is happening. Realize what it is you're striving for or what you want to represent and know the supply will meet the demand when you see this card. Whatever you choose will be the right choice.

The number three typically suggests the initial completion of a project or venture and in this case suggests a wedding celebration, the birth of a child, or the successful initial fulfillment of a goal. However, despite the completion or satisfaction offered by the number three, this card also suggests a new beginning; the celebration is only the start of a long and possibly difficult journey. Success. Friendship. Communication, enjoyment of others, celebration, music, pregnancy. Good fortune. Celebrations, happiness, re-unions, Parties and meetings which lead to love affairs and flirtations. Pregnancy or birth. Ills are haled. Attendance at weddings and christenings likely. Shared experience. All of the above are implied when we see this card in a spread.

This card also represents a fortunate end to a project or venture. It can mean a birth of a new project also. It portends great happiness as a result of a birth or marriage. Something conceived out of love comes to fruition. The three of cups is a card of abundant fertility, trust, harmony, maternity and the healing of ills. It also means attending a possible party or celebration.

Reversed

In relationship readings, the III of Cups reversed nearly always indicates a third person is involved, and typically, it is the querent who is that third person. When you see this card in a reading, look to the other cards in the reading also. if you see the VII of Swords, there is a likely betrayal of trust and getting away with something. If you see the V of Swords, it is likely that the querent already knows about the other relationship but is trying to ignore that it exists. If you see the Devil in the same spread then you need to think carefully about the nature of the relationships you are in; they are likely to be hedonistic and generally unhealthy to those involved. Pleasure turns to pain.

Beware of an old friend gossip. Don't over-indulge in food and drink. Abundance may turn to nothing and success may turn to ashes.

When the III of Cups shows in a spread reversed it can indicate that the person self indulges to excess. Selfishness and sexuality is also implied. Loss of happiness, loveless sex, unbridled passion, famine and illness associated with smoking and overeating are all possibilities when this card is reversed depending on the remaining spread. This card in reverse signals promiscuity. The reverse III of Cups also warns against obesity.

IV of Cups

Meaning Upright

The IV of Cups indicates a time of uncertainty and decision and a turning inward to find the Truth for which one is searching. External influences can be distracting and may not lead us to the goal we seek even if those influences purport to be of a spiritual nature. The IV of Cups means disappointment in someone or in a situation. You may become tired of the same old struggle that has been carried on too long in the past. The end result may include disappointment in the final result. One avenue of interpretation of the IV of Cups is that of apathy or indifference. Another interpretation is that of defensiveness. This card signals a pause. Discontent. Boredom. Tested relationships through negative attitudes. Considers an affair. A difficult situation caused by someone trying to do well. Stability in relationship. Familiarity breeds contempt. A new start needed to renew spark. New interests, activities and friends are needed. Tested relationships.

The IV of Cups suggests the person re-evaluate their life, situation and environment because familiarity breeds contempt as well as dissatisfaction and boredom. Nothing offered satisfies this person anymore. There is a need to search for a more stimulating way of life. This person is apathetic and dwells in the past. Love becomes to routine and familiar (The spark is gone). Happiness has reached its peak with the person or situation. This card can also mean the start of establishing a family.

Reversed

When we see this card reversed its implying a new relationship now possible. There is a desire for work and accomplishment and new goals. There is a good possibility that an offer will come your way, but you must work hard to go out and get it. You are missing an opportunity that is sitting right under your nose! Look around you to see opportunities you may have missed.

This card also tells the person that their ill health and fatigue is due to their overindulgences. In reverse the IV of Cups can also mean excesses of all kinds depending on where it is in the spread. It can also me that this person is totally overturning his current life style.

Depending on the spread it can mean rapid change creates new anxieties and excitement for excitement's sake brings little or just a fleeting pleasure. This card reversed also indicates the person has a low boredom threshold.

V of Cups

Meaning Upright

The V of Cups represent fulfillment or non-attainment of expected results. You may lose something, though it is insignificant in itself. Perhaps relations with friends or lovers have weak foundations. You'll be completely burned out and will want to quit or give up. You've done enough and won't want to do anymore. You and a relative (or very dear friend) will soon part, and you will be very sad. You want a friend or lover to return, or a REAL relationship based on tenderness and mutual enchantment. Nothing less. Something will replace or sublimate the emptiness you feel. This card portends sorrow and or loss of a loved one. The persons marriage is on verge of breaking up. Disillusionment with life. Possible inheritance, but not as much as expected.

This card pertains to "crying over spilled milk" and pessimism about the future. It often refers to a person who is having difficulty letting go of the past and benefiting from past mistakes. Emotional disappointment, (also in friendship) depression, anger (usually based on past experiences) - all exaggerated. Deep regrets, temporary delay. Loss of harmony, but love is still there. Someone has an unexpected reaction to the querent. Loss of relationship, hurt. This card urges you to stop crying and look in another direction for happiness. Get over hurt, and then pick up remaining cups and carry on.

Disappointment. You need to understand rejection and disappointment. You may feel that you must walk away from someone or something. Realize the ways your disappointment gains you experience that can help to ensure future success. When we see this card it is telling us to re-order and re-evaluate our priorities.

This card has to do with the difficulties entailed in a union or engagement that is either about to be lost or is lost already. It represents a loss or defeat and a dishonor that cannot be overcome. When we see this card we have to accept the inevitable and not curb futile belligerence. The V of Cups represent worries and regrets. Broken engagements lead to emotional letdowns. It also is a card representing emotional or monetary legacies.

Reversed

When we see the V of Cups reversed it is telling us of the return of hope, new alliances formed. Loved one could be returning to you so summon up your courage. The reversed position shows recovery from regret and an acceptance of the past. Now, the person realizes the full implications of the past and appreciates the lessons he learned from the experience. He may even recognize the value of the painful experience in the broader scheme of things in preparing him for later experiences. He is ready to pick up the remaining two cups that are full of the water of emotional growth and go on.

This card is about learning to be open and starting to take risks again. It is a card of a lingering sense of regret, nostalgia and bittersweet memories. However the card itself speaks of being hopeful for the future, getting over whatever you need to get over, and of seeing the sun peek through the clouds once again! If you have suffered a broken romance or marriage, this card signifies an end to the suffering, and a beginning to new loves and relationships, new interests, and new emotional outlets.

You are starting to engage with the inspiring, creative and feeling side of life again. This card in reverse represents a way of life being turned upside down or overturned. Depending on the spread it can mean false starts as well as unexpected worries from and unexpected source. A feeling of abandonment or loneliness as a result of bad luck are also portended when this card is reversed.

VI of Cups

Meaning

A keyword I have for this card is "remembering." Whether that be through nostalgia, news or a visit from the past. It implies thinking of another by giving a peace-offering or a gift (perhaps remembering someone's birthday). This card is one that talks about the past and memories. It portends the person is looking back for example; on childhood, happiness, enjoyment from before which have vanished. Meeting with a childhood acquaintance who has a gift for you, happiness and enjoyment come from the past, pleasant memories are all implied from seeing this card.

This card also signals; new surroundings and opportunities, possible inheritance. Pleasure from the past, happiness, balance and peace, memory or renewal of past, gifts, friendship. Success after struggle. Memory, links to the past (old friend or lover may turn up soon) Childhood. Past efforts to be rewarded. The answer of one's question lies in a similar situation in the past. Possibly a move of home, closer to origin. Sentimental value.

In general this card denotes harmony of past associations bringing present relationships. It can represent happiness from past efforts as well as pleasant memories and the realization of a dream. Depending on the spread this card means there are new elements entering the person's life which are linked to the past, which work through the present to create a future. Finally Joy. You need to experience child-like joy. The child you were still lives within you and must be cared for. Allow yourself positive, nostalgic memories of childhood, friends and family. If you can, spend time with younger people.

Reversed

The VI of Cups reversed can represent someone who is quite nostalgic, childlike, generous with love and affection, and, at times, naive. This person may unrealistically paint rosy ideas about love, relationships and marriage. Having impure or sneaky motives. Feeling jaded, cynical or bitter. Not taking time out to 'play'. Feeling abandoned and/or unloved.

This card reversed signals that the person is feeling that they have missed out on a happy and loving childhood. Encountering serious difficulties at a young age. An unhappy home life. An abusive parent or guardian. Child abuse. Family rifts and problems. And old friendship that turns sour. This card signals being told that you can't have children or a death of a child. Living in the past instead of the present. Disappointment over inheritance. Longing for the past that will never return.

This person is vain and has a sense of pride from their past accomplishments which is preventing them from succeeding in the now. Depending on the spread this person clings to the past and out dated habits and customs. They also have an exaggerated idea of nostalgia and the past.

VII of Cups

Meaning Upright

This card indicates that we are faced with a time of decision, that the images in our minds must be dealt with not only in our dreams but in the world of reality. The character in the VII of Cups is a dreamer who is able to see beauty and excitement as well as fearful trials and difficulties in the future. If we are constantly caught up in our own dreams, fantasies, and/or fears, we will never be able to move forward and make those dreams a reality or overcome those fears.

This card indicates that though dreaming is beautiful and provides inspiration for action, we must at some point abandon our "castles in the sky" and begin to build those castles in our real life. A choice must be made even though the apparent multiplicity of options seems to paralyze us with either fear or excessive anticipation. If you are unable to make a decision because of too many options, it may be time to carefully evaluate the pros and cons of each option and make a thoughtful choice.

The VII of Cups speaks of letting go. Letting go of a former relationship, workplace or project. When the VII of Cups appears, it is important to look carefully at how disordered your situation sometimes has become. It may have turned in a chaotic situation where some tightening may be necessary. It is easy to wish for something, but not so easy to make that wish come true. A choice, and a sacrifice will have to be made. You need to separate what is real from what is illusion. Protect against unclear or wishful Thinking. Learn the power of your sleeping and waking dreams. Avoid intoxication and escapism. Do not decide until you are sure.

This card portends one's imagination Working overtime and the inability to choose direction in life. This person lives though selfish indulgence in dreams instead of action. They have Illusory success and are habitually day dreaming. Make your priorities clear. Over indulgence, illusions, moods, negativity, "You get what you think of", imagination. Misuse of talent. Choices. A decision has to be made, lots of options to choose from. Make decision careful, all is not what it seems to be. Doorways of opportunity use intuition to know which one to go through. Pipe Dreams.

VII of cups is a wish card. Each of the cups are filled with wishes such as wealth, beauty, Peace, and a nice home (castle). You can also see that there is a cup with a snake and a cup with a demon. This is showing that wishes can go a rye. Many readers may consider this card a good omen. This card in reality can be a mixed blessing; be careful for what you wish for you may just get it, and with a price. As you can see that the cup standing for peace (olive branch) there is a skull. There may be peace but at what or whose cost? This card means that you have to think about your choices and options. There may be too many choices and opportunities present; which need careful consideration to avoid a grave judgment error. May refer to the choice of marriage and a few partner options to pick from. The person in question is being given a big opportunity but he has to be able to pick it out from the available choices he has. This card can also allude to a great mystical experience that the person has gone through or is going to go through that was very inspiring.

Reversed

Good use of determination and will. A definite project will be selected. This card could indicate an unwillingness to deal with the day-to-day reality of life, a caution to get your head out of the clouds. It can also mean that this person relies on false hopes instead of reality. Depending on the spread it can mean inaction means lost opportunities. Reversed this card means a decision is reached (when in reverse and based on the surrounding cards). It can also signal this person has a fear of success, is self deluded and indecisive.

VIII of Cups

Meaning Upright

The VIII of Cups Meaning includes overextended one's self to the point of exhaustion. This card cautions the person to slow down and take it slower before he gets totally burnt-out. Rejection of material life. Disappointment in love. Desire to leave material success for something higher. Wish is fulfilled but not to the degree you want it to. Seize the day to gain honor. It is a card indicating; retreat, withdrawal, self-pity, over-giving, over-extending. Honor your limits. This person uses too much caution, not enough faith, doubts about success. They Hesitate to think more positively, are fed-up and have an unjustified dissatisfaction. This card indicates a new path in life is what this person is seeking.

Don't be afraid to leave the past behind. There's plenty more in the world to see. Don't be disillusioned, the future promises to be brighter. Follow your heart, do what you desire. Disappointed with accomplishments, dissatisfied. Take a break and make a change. Weariness. The fluidity of water, i.e. the self, knows when, despite a situation being good, it is time to leave. This is especially to move in a direction which is more "air-like", more in touch with reality, i.e. away from emotions.

The astrological correspondence for this card is Saturn in Pisces. Saturn is the planet of discipline. Pisces is the sign of the fish-- water; emotions.

In a relationship reading, the VIII of Cups highlights that you would ideally like to escape all the emotional issues that surround the relationship, and carry on as if you were in a perfect partnership. You would like to be able to turn your back on any of your past issues, and re-establish a new relationship together. However, deep down, you know that these issues which will continue to plague the relationship if they go undressed.

This card can also indicate that there is a turning point where links in the past are severed. This is due to the fact that they are out dated for the person. It also tells of the person walking away from established relationships and affection. They do this in order to facilitate progress to newer and deeper things. Depending on the spread this card can also mean a change of perspective or viewpoint. The VIII of Cups card also deals with issues of security and attachment.

Reversed

Jealousy is in the air. A message you have been waiting to hear has not yet shown up. Do not become too bold or to courageous. Business slows down and your love life ends up at a standstill When this card shows up in the reverse someone has abandoned that which is well established for an impossible dream. Depending where it shows up in the spread in reverse this card means fantasy and risk. It also implies the person is reckless and restless.

IX of Cups

Meaning Upright

The IX of Cups indicates good health and much success. There will be a situation which will provide for your best interests. Material gains could be part of your attainment as well as emotional support in life. Your work will start off bright, then turn dark, and then bright again. Don't worry, after a slight retrograde, you'll see material gain or a good outcome. An emotional issue concerning the care or treatment of another will be discussed.

Nines represent personal integrity and completion, or the final stage of development. Nine is associated with the Moon - therefore dreams and delusions play a role in cards numbered nine. This final stage may bring certain problems with it, and past experiences and methods of coping become important here and are an intrinsic part of the meaning attached to the nines. The Nine of Cups represents fulfillment, stability and advancement. This is a card of great success, especially material success. It represents triumph, victory, and financial well-being. This card signals enjoyment of good personal relationships, love and friendship, as well as comfortable material circumstances are indicated. It is a card that reflects happiness which is either health, finances, work, luck, love or relationship. Your desires will be fulfilled, and this fulfillment will bring with it much satisfaction and contentment. This is the traditional wish card, so whatever the querent desires here can be theirs -- however, everything does come with a price, and they should be careful what they wish for because they are likely to receive it!

Achievement, satisfaction, wishes fulfilled, self-indulgence, happiness are all implied with this card. The Wish Card. Excellent social life. Parties, good friends and fun. Good health, happiness and popularity. Fulfilling relationships, ease of communication. Contentment. This card is an omen for an assured future. It indicates the person will have satisfaction, contentment and physical well being. It also is an indication of overcoming difficulties. It tells of emotional stability and a safe outlook. This persons inner being is so secure that it radiates in their aura as one of good will. The card IX of Cups indicates this person is liberal, has a generous spirit and feelings of well being.

Reversed

When IX of Cups is reversed, it suggests that you may be disappointed that your wishes are not materializing. Perhaps there are a lot of desires that you have and hope for from this life, but there is some frustration because these aren't being fulfilled. In the reversed position, the Nine of Cups can point to disappointments due to imperfections and mistakes, smugness, overindulgence, greed, superficial or materialistic values, shallowness, gluttony, and excessive preoccupation with gratifying your own desires, often times at the expense of the needs of others.

It can also indicate ill-fortune due to over-indulgence in food, alcohol, or drugs and the consequences that come with it. Reversed this card also point to a wish that is not yet fulfilled, perhaps because it is desired too intensely or the querent is sabotaging their own efforts. Sometimes this card shows up reversed when the person being read to is going through a depression or lack of self-worth. A love of sensual pleasure is indicated along with a lack of material goods and money. Overindulgence in food and drink. Depending on the spread this card implies the person is falling into error, complacency, vanity and self indulgence. This person is short of money due to overspending or it can indicate a loss of credit or credit cards. They tend to be over sentimental and overlook others faults. Because of this they are used and abused for their hospitality. Their kindness is taken for weakness.

X of Cups

Meaning Upright

The X of Cups is indicative of a good family life. Happiness, joy and contentment will dominate your life when this card pops up in a spread. The time will be made for the enjoyment of pleasures which may be shared with another person whom you love. There will be correspondence connected with your work that will involve mail, phone calls, or special application. You will get a long distance call from a relative, or you will make one.

The X of Cups represents a satisfaction and joy much like that experienced in the IX of Cups. The difference, however, should be quite clear. The IX of Cups represented personal attainment whereas the X of Cups represents the satisfying fulfillment of love in relationship with another. This card is a very positive card in terms of relationships and may indicate either the beginning of a new, very happy relationship, or the ultimate satisfaction of a long-term relationship. Commitment and love are the requirements of such satisfaction, yet this card promises that with the required effort a lasting love can be built. Happy family life. True friendships. Lasting happiness inspired from above. Perfection of love and friendship. Success.

You need to be more aware of how successful and respected you are. You will never gain more than you have now until you empower yourself by appreciating what you have done. Success is really how you define it. This card signals peace, domestic happiness, wholeness, completion, optimism. Successful development. Friendship, companionship. Family happiness that will last. Group activities denoting fun. Everything will work out for the best. Happy endings. This is a card representing lasting happiness and security.

The person has a good reputation and honor. They also have true friendship and a happy family life. X of Cups means perfect love and concord between people. The person's search for fulfillment is one of success. It also signifies a secure and peaceful environment.

Reversed

The X of Cups reversed signals either a family quarrel or a loss of friendship. Chance of betrayal. Young people may turn against their parents. It tells us that someone manipulates society for personal gain. This card reversed can also indicate a sudden violent eruption of an ordered environment or ordered routine. It indicates that someone has anti social actions. It is also a sign of births or new adolescents emerging.

Page of Cups

Meaning Upright

A physical description - light brown hair, fair complexion, blue eyes. Good Looking, pretty.

Personality traits - studious youth, loving friend, not a lover, could be a person with a youthful frame of mind. Helpful, very reliable, but not strong, and could be dependent on Querent. They offer service to you, want to be of help. Gentle, loving, artistic, insightful. Girl - tomboyish, boy - feminine. Gentleness, sweetness, kindness. Someone who is interested in poetry and the arts, dreamy at times yet courageous when courage is needed.

This card signals news, perhaps the birth of a child. Someone is emotionally vulnerable and needs affection. The energy of this card is almost always gentle and youthful. The flavor of this card reeks of creativity and emotions. Depending on the other cards with it and its placement in the spread it could also mean: news of a birth; a wonderful idea or plan; a message of emotions; this could be a pregnancy card; someone playful like pixies, elves and sprites; a social invitation; an invite to a seafood restaurant; a trip to the beach; a young person who like to fish; someone who swims like a fish; a budding poet, an artist; an interior decorator; a professional psychic; an old fashioned love song; a romantic film i.e. "Gone With The Wind"; a florist; a delivery of flowers for someone; someone who communes with the dolphins; a romantic writer; Harlequin Romance novels; seashell collector; someone who carries a deep love of history; a gay person; love letters in the sand.

This card can also represent the querent or someone in the querent's life who is sweet, graceful, sensitive, charming and highly emotional and creative. Someone who is moved by beauty. Most of the time it represents a child, or child-like adult.

The Page of Cups can be used to identify an impressionable or emotional young person. When the Page of Cups represents a new event, the querent will react to this event in an emotional manner.

In a reading regarding spiritual issues, the Page could indicate the beginning of a spiritual journey undertaken for emotional reasons. The Page could also indicate a new beginning of an emotional nature the start of a new relationship, a creative idea, an exciting new project.This card can also represent the querent or someone in the querent's life who is sweet, graceful, sensitive, charming and highly emotional and creative. Someone who is moved by beauty. Most of the time it represents a child, or child-like adult. This card also represents the imagination. It can signal a time is needed for quiet reflection. Depending on the surrounding cards it can announce a engagement or marriage. This person is very knowledgeable and gives it away freely. They are also gifted with a lot of foresight.

Reversed

It is a card of someone who is immature or has emotional troubles. It can depict a person who is escaping through drugs or alcohol, or someone who is running away from reality and living in his own world. This is a person who is emotionally insecure and unable to conduct healthy relationships. He expects too much and gives too little. He is lacking in self-love and self-acceptance, and may be emotionally abusive. This person has rampant and unfocused emotions, and may therefore imagines a lot and gets his feeling hurt without reason. He is suspicious, self-doubting, insincere, selfish and easily depressed. Selfishness and love of luxury. Little desire to create.

Depending on the rest of the spread this card in reverse also indicates a deception is about to be revealed. This person cannot make commitments and is shallow as well as self indulgent. They are a jack of all trades but will only shallow surface knowledge. This person schemes and connives and does not share his knowledge. He loves beauty but does not apply himself to become an artist. This card reversed indicates a lazy person who lies and partakes in harmful gossip.

Knight of Cups

Meaning Upright

Physical description - light brown hair, fair complexion. May be a "traveler." Casual appearance. Well traveled.

Personality traits - temporary enthusiasms. Enthusiastic, passionate, amiable. Often poetic and graceful.

The Knight of the Cups denotes the arrival of someone or something. An invitation or request may be received. An appeal or proposal may be made on behalf of someone else through a third party. This person wants something so bad, they think it will come to pass if they close their eyes to the possibility of defeat and hope for the best. They may also want to change your residence and will be advancing towards their goals. Expect positive changes because things are Looking up.

Remember, Cups are the suit of emotions. The Knight is looking to his emotions to provide a map. He is the person who is ruled by his heart rather than his head. When faced with a decision, this person will always go with what his heart tells him, whether it is logical or not. A young man of high intelligence. A romantic dreamer. If querent is a woman, she may be falling in love with such a man. The coming or going of a matter involving emotions. A young man is friendly toward the querent. A bringer of advice and a message. This card represents change and exciting news particularly romantic in nature. It is a card of invitations, opportunities and offers. The person this card represents brings those things. He is also bored and needs constant stimulation. He is also refined and artistic. An amiable person but a dreamer who is easily led and gets discouraged fast. He is intelligent and tries to maintain high principals.

Reversed

The Knight of Cups reversed allows his emotions too much control over him. He may be moody, jealous, emotional to point of incapacity. He may jump to conclusions before getting all the facts. If this card shows up reversed, either look at yourself and at how you are acting, or realize that the person involved may be acting from his emotions rather than from any form of logic.

The Knight of Cups reversed indicates a situation which was initially incredibly appealing, romantic and exciting, but which later turns out to be something very different, and one walks away feeling quite disappointed. It's like wearing the rose-colored glasses, or going through the honeymoon period, only to come out realizing that the situation is quite different to what you thought. Beware of trickery and fraud. Sensuality, idleness. A treacherous deceitful young man. emotional harm to querent.

This person is unreliable and reckless. In reverse depending on the spread the meaning is suggesting fraud, embezzlement, false promises and trickery. This person is an inbred liar. They have trouble distinguishing where the lie ends and truth begins.

Queen of Cups

Meaning Upright:

Physical description - light brown hair, fair complexion, beautiful woman, expressive eyes, sensuous lips.

Personality traits - warm, loving, sociable. Good-natured woman, devoted and honest. Sympathetic, sociable, artistically gifted. Very imaginative, honest, loyal.

The Queen of Cups is an adored woman. She is admired for her fairness and honesty. She is warm-hearted and a good friend. She indicates that a woman may assist you in your situation. Queen of Cups is a nurturing personality. She genuinely cares about the well-being of other people. She could be a mother, or a mother figure.

The Queen gives freely to others. She is creative, and highly intuitive. You may be called upon to help, or care for, another. You will be glad to help, but make sure you take care of yourself as well. You should pay close attention to your inner voice. Trust your intuition. You might feel a burst of creativity, or become involved in a creative project. Caring, sensitive to the feelings of others, compassion, kind to animals and children, intuitive, emotional, heart on the sleeve, understanding, responds to the unconscious, spiritual, patience, unconditional love and acceptance, telepathic, reverence for life, mature love relationships, sincerity, has well developed 6th sense, gentle, motherly, good listener, empathy, good in matters of the heart, has an inner guide, psychic ability, oneness with all people, mysterious, devoted, helps those in need, tender-hearted, experiences life as sacred, other worldly, ethereal beauty, loves fantasy, easily influenced, passionate, loyal, self acceptance, ability to listen to feelings, perceptive, imaginative, gift of prophesy are all implications of this card.

This person Loves art, poetry and music, has nurturing and protective energy, inner visions and dreams, the muse who inspires, enchantress, mythology, power of the unconscious, divine inspiration, mother love, collective unconscious, depths of the psyche, mysterious feminine, seductive, pay attention to the anima, fragile and easily hurt. She can also be unfathomable, still waters run deep, open in showing feelings, sympathetic ear and a shoulder to cry on, keeps emotions under control, dislikes thoughtless and inappropriate behavior, strong moral sense, tranquil, compelling.

This is a happy card that represents balance and harmony. It also indicates success that is achieved due to a good imagination. This woman is very imaginative as well as artistically gifted. She is romantic, has a affectionate outlook and creates a worldly atmosphere around her. She lacks common sense but is highly intuitive, psychic and dreamlike. Other people and environments are sources of easy influence for her.

Reversed

When this card is reversed it signals your imagination runs away with you. You mean well but you cannot be relied on. Pleasure and happiness turn bitter. Untrustworthy woman is near. Out of touch with feelings, overwhelmed by emotion, anxious, unstable, brooding, suspicious, erratic behavior, fickle, moody, lay, unfaithful, self indulgent, overly secretive, cold and calculating, irrational, gossip, hurts others, perverse, bitter, unable to relate to children, unable to give nurturing. This woman changes her feelings and opinions without reason or cause. She can be perverse and given to hysteria. She can lead others to a destruction in pursuit of her idle fantasies. She cannot be relied or depended on at all.

King of Cups

Meaning Upright

Physical description - light brown hair, fair complexion. Clear liquid eyes. Older man, business man in responsible position. A kindly gentleman. A fatherly figure.

Personality traits - you may not understand him, but you can trust him. He has achieved something in life. Sociable, loving, sensuous. Intelligence combined with strong intuition. Enjoys comforts of life. Love of arts. Responsible and generous.

The King of Cups, like all the court cards in the suit of Cups, represents emotion, creativity, and the unconscious. Unlike the preceding Three court cards, however, the King of Cups expresses much more restraint in his emotional state. He is a master of his own feelings, and remains in control of his emotions. Not to say that he represses those feelings and sentiments; on the contrary, the King of Cups represents the balance between the emotions and the intellect.

He is a master of compassion and kindness and his card often indicates strong bonds in a relationship based on temperance and understanding. A man of business, law or divinity, kind, considerate, and willing to take responsibility. He is interested in the arts and sciences and enjoys quiet power. It can mean someone displays paternal feelings toward you.

The King of Cups shows you generosity, graciousness, love, calmness, caring and will give you his healing ways. He has power in the business world and loves law and order. You would love him to be your doctor. If there were a crisis at hand, we should all hope to have this person near. Generosity, understanding, dignity, calmness, aura of power, deep reflective spirit, religious feelings, goes to the point, knowledgeable, eloquent, feelings under control, alchemist, moral courage, willing to do what is needed, passionate, committed to social change, fertility and transformation, regal, enthusiastic, expansive, emotional security, inspirational, literate, empathetic, nurturing, fatherly, wisdom, psychic healer, offers assistance, reliable, wisdom, wounded healer, gracious, loving, loves law and order, good in a crisis, openness, acceptance, health and wholeness, warm hearted, helpful, takes initiative, ability to live one's ideals.

Caring, mediator, professional, secretive, negotiator, empathetic, cultured, keeps feelings to himself, good in an emerging dynamic, able to bring ideas to fruition, counselor, confidant, considerate, resolved, mature, imaginative, protector, sympathetic, ambivalent nature, paradoxical, personal relationships, concern for others, self denying, kind, good listener, provider, moody, sophisticated, quiet and deep, sensitive, artistic, compassionate, communicates feelings, romantic, poet, guardian of hidden mysteries, harmonious relationships, community respect, religious, adaptable, creative thinker, sensual, spiritual, practitioner of alternative medicine, tranquility, intimacy, interpreter of dreams and visions, thoughtful, devotion and service, gentle touch.

This is the type of man that commands respect but not love. He is a natural born manipulator. He has achieved his position in life by the use of his brains not his brawn. He avoids taking people into he confidence and prefers to work in secret behind the scenes. He craves power, he is driven by hidden motives and people around him both fear and distrust him.

Reversed

A powerful man but likely to be double dealing. A crafty violent nature. A scandal is in the air, be careful. This card signals someone who is unfeeling, sleazy, uncultured, barbaric, insecure, immature, unimaginative, double dealer, forked tongue, false friend, worthless advice, con artist, deceptive, dishonest, play acting, insecure, manipulative, toys with emotions, lazy, exploitive, addictive personality, violent, treacherous ruler, untrustworthy. This man has no morality and his only allegiance is to himself. He involves his associates in scandal, corruption, vice, dishonesty and evil just like him. With him the saying still water run deep is a pre warning as well as all the glitters is not gold.

Chapter 7

Pentacles

The Pentacle Suit in the Tarot deck corresponds to the Diamonds in the regular playing card deck. Pentacles represent material possessions, industry, business, commerce, trade, finances, and security. They deal with the external level of consciousness. Pentacles mirror the outer situations of your health, finances, work, and creativity.

Pentacles represent the Earth signs of Taurus, Virgo, and Capricorn. Earth covers the mundane material things of life, property, money, home and nature. Also manifestation, realization, proof and prosperity. Pentacle symbols include the bull, gnomes, black hair, and black eyes. Pentacles are indicative of Autumn, or "years" in "time" questions in tarot.

Ace of Pentacles

Meaning Upright:

The Ace of pentacles indicates great wealth and happiness. The happiness may be the result of the receipt of something long desired. The wealth, however, need not have a monetary value. Some of the greatest gifts of life cannot be bought.

The Ace of Pentacles, like the Aces of the other suits, is representative of new beginnings, fresh energy, and inspiration. In this case, the pentacles are analogous to the alchemical element of earth, and therefore symbolize the material world and things associated with matter and the body. Pentacles also represent money and the financial concerns which we may have at the time of our reading.

The Ace of Pentacles can suggest that we need to introduce something new into the equation. Rather than let things remain as they are, and hope they work themselves out, the Ace suggests we throw something new into the mix. What should that be? Well, take a few minutes to consider. If it were easy, you'd have already tried it. If it were safe and accepted, you'd have already tried it. Why not consider something out-of-character or something you'd normally never do. That doesn't mean dancing naked on Main Street, just something that you might not ordinarily do, or get around to doing.

The Ace of Pentacles indicates the beginning of new energy and revitalized interest in the material or financial areas of your life. This card may represent the beginning of new investments or the willingness to undertake a new business venture. There is also the possible indication of a legacy or influx of money from an unexpected source.

The Ace of Pentacles heralds a feeling of prosperity and abundance and should be accepted joyfully; it is a very positive card in general. The Ace of Pentacles is also a sign that you will be able to make your dreams real. Your ideas are ready to be turned into something tangible. Figure out what will work and make it a reality. You can now attract all the wealth you need to get your projects going. Tap into the material force of the Ace of Pentacles, you will prosper, and all your enterprises will flourish.

When we see the Ace of Pentacles we know that there will be financial change for the better. The financial changes include material comforts,, wealth, possessions and appreciation for the good things in life. This card also means good health. This represents the essence and riches of the earth element.

Prosperity, fertility, generosity, fruits of labor, material pleasures, new financial ventures, burst of energy for material creation, creative vision, crafts, ambition, craftsman, skills, success, material achievement, security, science, available money, productivity, foundation, physical delight, acquisition are all associated with the Ace of Pentacles. As are manifestation, protection, endurance, reproduction, stability, constant, perfection, contentment, beauty, helping hand, windfall, security, good fortune, comfort, recognition, promotion, reward for hard work, good health, pennies from heaven, bountiful, beneficial, profit, agreeable, wealth, possessions, property, new job, new baby, new life pattern, birth.

Wisdom, spiritual treasures, gemstones, fulfillment, sensation, instinct, contentment, happiness, news, worldliness, fortune, success, recognition, being at the apes, bliss, attainment, happy marriage, happy home, inheritance, ecstasy, freedom, confidence, beauty of nature, inauguration, spiritual riches, sovereignty, sustenance, earthy, optimistic, bright prospects, benign, beginning a venture, fresh start, charge of physical energy, financial breakthrough, beginning of time, flowering, wholeness, wellness, balanced truths, nurturing and wholesome are all heralded by this card.

It tells you that the end of a process is near. After the initial excitement of a new idea (wands), the inner turmoil of it all (cups), the struggle with it in the outside world (swords), now the time has come that your ideas will be materialized. There will be a lot of hard work involved (this is pentacles after all), but it is an exciting card that helps you manifest your ideas in the outside world.

Reversed:

Taking what one hasn't earned, corruption, greed, money can't buy happiness, stubborn, confused, carried away by passion, materialism, clinging to the past, fear of death, inability or refusal to understand cause and effect, overlooked for promotion, extravagance are all implied when we see this card reversed. When we see the Ace of Pentacles reversed in a spread its telling us about greed, the person in the spread depends on physical pleasures for happiness, avarice, the person in the spread is miserly and it talks of materialism. This person lacks imagination and someone fears death.

II of Pentacles

Meaning:

The II of Pentacles indicate there are problems and difficulties in the future. There may be obstacles erected which hinder the attainment of what you wish to pursue or obtain in life. The situation may cause undue worry or social embarrassment. Like the picture of the person is trying to juggle the different aspects of their life to make it work. This card follows upon the initial energy of the Ace of Pentacles in which we are psychologically prepared to embrace success and prosperity.

The twos of any suit typically represent the conflicts inherent in the opposites, and any pending decisions which must be made. In the Two of Pentacles, we find an individual whose consciousness, represented by the waters, is tossed by ostensibly conflicting interests. For example, if the Ace of Pentacles represents the beginnings of a new business or financial venture, the Two represents the need to balance that venture with other important areas of life such as family, friends, and even our own physical, mental, and spiritual well-being. This card indicates the necessity for balance between opposing desires and interests. Though it is necessary to take such circumstances seriously, the Two of Pentacles nevertheless indicates that our psychological health may ultimately be better served if we are able to temper our seriousness and drive for success with a sense of humor and the childlike ability to enjoy ourselves despite our outward condition. The sea of our lives will always be uncertain, yet if we can produce balance and harmony among all the demands upon us we will ultimately live happily and in prosperity.

When we see this card we know there are vast change and fluctuations for the person in question. This person has to balance their skills when they plan for the future. This card is also a warning not to use your credit card, do not buy things on it. The changes and movement this card talks about are things in the form of news, journeys, communication, money and material preoccupation. When we see this card pop up its telling us we have to use our knowledge skillfully to affect continued success and to be able to manipulate life's rules to our benefit. An established business has to be handled with care now.

Reversed:

The II of Pentacles reversed is an indicator that you are struggling to juggle all of your commitments. To overcome this, you need to do is prioritize and manage your time carefully.

Invest your time only in those activities that have the most value to your life. Additionally, the II of Pentacles reversed indicates that you are finding it hard to manage your finances and your cash flow may be quite unpredictable. Now is the time to start a budget and stick to it. When we see this card reversed its telling us there is fickleness around us or that we ourselves are fickle. It warns of reckless elation and discounting the warning at the expense of impending trouble. Reversed this card tells of dept, and over indulgence in physical pleasures it can indicate drunkenness as well. There is an inability to complete a project.

III of Pentacles

Meaning Upright

The III of Pentacles, like the Threes in the other suits, represents the initial completion of a goal or plan. In this case, the Three seems to imply the fulfillment and manifestation of a creative venture, business, or building project. The inspiration of the one is beginning to be concreted in the material world, and the decisions of the two have been made successfully. An initial satisfaction is now being enjoyed and the project is well underway. However, the Three does not indicate the final completion of any project or venture but rather just the beginning.

The Number Three signifies the first manifestation of a creative union. Just as a child is born to the union of two lovers, the creative idea is finally born when the conflicting desires of the heart are in equilibrium and when fear of failure is balanced with enthusiasm for potential success. The message of the Three of Pentacles, therefore, is primarily one of encouragement. Work. You need to do work that is satisfying to you. Skill. Work with others. Satisfaction. Practicality. Clear on priorities and commitments. Make most of talents, increase success through continuation of craft or educational pursuit. Promotion or increase. Use of skills to make profit. High achievement. Rising above friends and opponents equally. Being a subject of envy. Perhaps a move of house. Intellectual property. Practical work, done consciously and with commitment may serve as the vehicle for self-development. Plans.

The III of Pentacles has all the skill necessary to accomplish your goals in life. You will have the ability to succeed in all your ventures. Want to get things accomplished and to improve the quality of your life or your work. You will have to revamp, redirect or make some alteration in your current work or plans. When we see this card in a spread it means success through hard work and one's hard efforts. It can also mean a gain of material and finances. This is a card implying that educating one's self will take them far, as well as upgrading the knowledge and skills they already have. III of Pentacles also represents the craftsmen or merchant. This card tells you that if you apply your skills in work you will be successful, it will be both awarded and appreciated. When we see this card it is saying to us that this is a good time to start a project or that you will receive help in a business.

Reversed

The III of Pentacles reversed signifies that you are seeking more respect in the workplace. You have had to be polite and listen to the opinions and feedback of your superiors, but now you seem to be growing restless with always taking the advice, rather than giving it.

In a career reading, you want to work in an environment where you have the chance to voice your own opinion and be heard, where you are seen as the expert or the leader. You may also be seeking new colleagues who bring with them new knowledge, so as to create a more synergistic team environment.

The reversed III of Pentacles can also indicate a lack of teamwork, whereby people are acting in competition with each other, trying to appear the most knowledgeable. It also indicates that your skills are not up to par and you need to learn more to succeed. When this card appears reversed it is telling us of a miserly person, one who has fear of loss so as a result they miss opportunities. This person is obstinate, conceited and or prejudice and because of that, they will not heed advice given to them. This card in reverse is also saying that the efforts one puts into something will not be rewarded; the yields are disappointing.

IV of Pentacles

Meaning Upright

The IV of pentacles represents a person who will not share anything in his life with other people. When assistance is needed, he will turn his back on the situation. Four of Pentacles indicates one of the dangers of prosperity: the temptation to value money far above its real worth. If wealth and financial success lead to a miserly or ungenerous attitude, then our psychological energy is in a closed or "contracted" state wherein nothing is perceived to have value other than money. This attitude is of course an expression of extreme attachment to the things of this world and is unhealthy in the long run simply because it is such an extreme point of view.

The IV of Pentacles indicates a person who is financially stable and secure with solid investments. This person is very conservative about money and is not inclined to gamble in financial matters. He is very protective of what he has and slowly and steadily increases his net worth through saving money and safe investments. He is self-sufficient both financially and emotionally, for he often equates money with emotional security. The Four is the card of the miser. His material possessions are on his head, representing that his thoughts are all about his "stuff". They are in his arms, indicating that they are not free to do anything else with his life. He can't go anywhere because his feet are busy holding the coins down. In other words, this man is so tied up with his possessions, that he can't do anything else. His possessions ARE his life. This is sad. Depending on where this card falls in a spread, it could be telling you to let go a little bit, and enjoy the other side of life (this is the card of the workaholic), or it could be telling you to tighten up a bit and not throw your money away.

It could indicate a need to tighten your belt a little bit. Look at where it falls and the cards that surround it to get the true meaning here. Possessiveness. You need to hold on to what you have. Manage and guard it carefully. Things must be put in order and in proper perspective. Reflect on your self-worth and what is valuable to you. It is time to think like an executive. On the other hand this card represents awareness of personal value and worth. Stability, comfort and practical security. Set and know limits.

Depending on the spread this card can signal that you could get good news from a woman, or "feminine" source.

Possessions. Material stability. Financial problems will be overcome.. Money in bank. ownership. Structure, either through material things, or by turning emotional and mental energy inwards. Selfishness (which might be precisely what is needed). Dependence on material comforts and security. Need for personal security. Blockage. Along with material and financial security this card indicates an increase of power and authority in relation to business, influence and wealth.

Overcoming financial and business obstacles is portended if this card appears. Depending on the spread it can mean a promotion. This card is telling someone that they do not need to use force to achieve the law and order they seek. It can actually be done through negotiation.

Reversed

Here, the conservatism of the IV of Pentacles has turned to greed and stinginess. The client is haunted by a fear of poverty which impels him to be grasping and materialistic. He is extremely defensive and self-protective materially and emotionally, fearful of opening up and trusting other people. This card relates to poverty conscientiousness, no matter how much money that person has. There is a lack of ability to delegate work and the bureaucracy is destroying the individual incentive and effort. Greed is indicated when this card is reversed. This person has a fear of losing what is familiar to them as well as what they established so as a result they are in opposition to any change now.

 **V of Pentacles**

Meaning Upright

The V of Pentacles may literally augur a time of financial strife and this possibility must be considered. However, other meanings of this card arise in connection to your psychological state at the time of the reading and your attitudes and expectations about money. Just as the IV of Pentacles indicated a psychological attachment to money and a tendency to overvalue this means of exchange, the V of Pentacles is also likely to indicate an inner difficulty with your relationship to money and material things. This card may therefore indicate a lack of confidence which is reflected in your self-judgment.

If money becomes the primary motivating force in life and the gauge by which we judge our worth, the lack of its abundance may produce anxiety and a sense of being excluded from the good things money can provide. In addition, if we encounter financial difficulties such as the loss of employment or an investment gone sour, we may fall into the trap of losing faith in our ability to recreate a positive financial situation for ourselves.

The V of Pentacles indicates failure and loss. This is applied more with regard to material loss than personal losses. You will experience troubles, dissension and possible loss in your work or career, as well as difficult dealings with others; and/or a heated debate over papers or contractual agreements. Someone in your family will be unhappy about their finances, partner or an infidelity. The trouble is that you will be too emotionally exhausted to help or lend any comfort.

This cad in reverse signals anxiety. You need to learn to cope with stress and anxiety. Worries can paralyze your actions until you face their source, focus on the present and do what you can with what you have now. Stress management is a vital concern. This card depending on the spread can also mean a divorce. There us a redundancy with the person. In any case this card is a definite warning of impending money troubles. But, depending on the spread it can mean a restriction in one area may actually open doors in another. Also depending on the spread this card can mean legal difficulties.

Reversed

The V of Pentacles reversed is about an end to difficult times. As the V of Pentacles in the upright position is about loneliness, despair, loss, rejection, hardship and abandonment, the reversed V of Pentacles signifies that this difficult period is coming to an end. You may be starting to feel as if life is worth living again and starting to regain your self-confidence. If you have experienced severe monetary problems or illness, these situations, too, are easing.

Reversed this card signals a time for relief and breathing easier are at hand. When we see the V of Pentacles reversed in a spread on of the first things it is telling us of is this person may have been unemployed for a long time and there is no success in this person's life. This card indicates poverty and destitution. When we see this card reversed depending on the surrounding cards it is saying that part of the reason the person is in this predicament is because of their stubbornness and lack of imagination.

VI of Pentacles

Meaning

The VI of Pentacles means balance and giving with regard to money and security. The giving of gifts and possessions. If describing a person it is someone who is generous and gives to charity. The six of pentacles is the money in-money out card. It is often giving someone a loan, or a gift of money, you get some you give it away and it comes back to you. it can also be an act of charity, money is not stagnant with the card, it is moving. But be careful not to deplete your resources here. This can also be giving of yourself, a volunteer position or something like that. Also you could be on the receiving end of a gift like this with this card. The VI of Pentacles will provide generosity and kindness to your situation resulting in gain for you.

This card signals another person will contribute to your efforts resulting in your success. Material gain may be indicated. Want what's rightfully or legally yours to be given back or to be reinstated in your profession or status. There ARE answers available and the key to solving problems is to stop thinking about them. This card follows appropriately upon the difficulties expressed in the V of Pentacles.

As in the VI of Pentacles, you as the questioner may be represented either by the rich merchant or by the beggars at his feet. In any case, there is a sense of peace and happiness about this card because it indicates the ending of the tribulation expressed by the five. The merchant represents not only the attainment of prosperity and financial stability, but also the experience of psychological peace in your relationship to money. This card signals Prosperity. Success. Physical attainment/accomplishment. Charitable attitude, sensitivity to others needs, sharing resources. Generosity. Money put to good use. Help from someone. Sharing, generosity and charity. Domination/submission, hierarchy. A force that holds together or reconciles the opposites in life.

When we see this card in a spread it is telling us about solvency in material affairs. It indicates a clearance of debts as well as using one's good fortune to benefit others. Depending on the cards position it indicates repaying a debt or a favor returned. This card also symbolizes charity, patronage, sympathy and a kind heart.

Reversed

Reversed, the VI of Pentacles can indicate theft, stealing of possessions or being unfair in financial affairs. Being cheated or used. In a relationship reading it can mean that one person is dominate over the other. There is a lack of real closeness. In reverse this card indicates recklessness and carless behavior with money. It also signifies loss of money through recklessness, theft or a deception as in being conned. Depending where it is in the spread it can also imply extravagance.

VII of Pentacles

Meaning Upright

The VII of Pentacles indicates success in all endeavors which require much time and effort. Despite the difficulty, your efforts will result in forthcoming rewards. You'll be dissatisfied with your progress and will experience anxiety about your business or financial state, and will want to be much more successful or solvent. You may be spending some somber times at home. Frustration. You need to cope with frustration. If hard work has not paid off as you planned, remember that expectations are almost always unreasonable. There are no guarantees. Be grateful, focus on the present and do what you can with what you have. The VII of Pentacles portrays a young man taking a rest from the difficult work of harvesting his abundant crop. He gazes meditatively at the pentacles hanging from the rich greenery of the thicket in which he works and seems to be contemplating the value of his efforts. If this card follows upon the VI of Pentacles it indicates the ending of a difficult period of financial or material difficulty.

In the VII of Pentacles, the situation is completely reversed and we now experience the rewards of hard work and effort. However, there is a decision looming in the air and this choice is at the root of the young man's contemplative expression. The question at hand is simply whether the rewards of hard work are in fact worth the effort to acquire them. It is often at the time of our greatest success that we realize what we desired so strongly is in fact somewhat disappointing.

This card indicates frustration. You need to cope with frustration. If hard work has not paid off as you planned, remember that expectations are almost always unreasonable. There are no guarantees. Be grateful, focus on the present and do what you can with what you have. Profit, re-evaluation, re-direction, business enterprise - period of growth, consider possibilities. Fear of failure/success. Planning, slow growth. Long term plans will reach fruition, but patience is needed.

In a reading, this card may mean fear of failure; delays; assessing past mistakes in order to learn from them; frustration, definitely, but learning a lesson from it; impotence, yes, from fear. When we see this card depending on the spread it can imply that current projects could fail. This card warns that you should not rest on the laurels now for you to have success you have to put in hard work at this time. Success is possible but you have to grab on to it first. The effort that you put in the past is now wasted because you are being inert. If you are doing charitable work at the moment there will be no rewards for doing so.

Reversed

The VII of Pentacles reversed indicates that even though you may continue to invest a lot of energy into a specific situation, you may not reap the rewards you are looking for. The VII of Pentacles reversed calls on you to prioritize your activities very carefully. You need to do a cost-benefit analysis on the major tasks involved to bring your project to fruition as there are certainly a number of tasks that are currently taking a lot of your time and energy but are not bearing the rewards you are seeking. Take stock of what you still need to do and focus only on those things that will get you to where you want to be.

When we see this card reversed it is telling us we induce our own worries over money. The reversed VII of Pentacles in a spread can mean bankruptcy, a person who gambles and talks of promising circumstances that end in failure. Reversed this is a card of financial insecurity.

VIII of Pentacles

Meaning Upright:

The VIII of Pentacles is the card of apprenticeship. While the seven indicates a time of decision and the revaluation of our financial situation, the eight indicates that a decision has been made and a new creative venture is underway. An apprenticeship is a time of learning new skills, a time of beginning something which one has not previously done. In this sense, the VIII of Pentacles indicates that you are experiencing or about to experience a change or new beginning in terms of work, education, or financial circumstances.

However, unlike many of the other cards indicating change or renewal, the VIII of Pentacles symbolizes a concentrated determination to master the new skill being learned. The VIII of Pentacles represents the single-minded effort of someone who has consciously chosen a new career path or creative undertaking. This card is the herald of success through perseverance and initiative as opposed to luck or the generosity of others, as is indicated in the VI of Pentacles. If you encounter this card in a reading and are not currently engaged in the active pursuit of your goals, it may be time to ask yourself what you could learn or create to better yourself or your circumstances.

If you are already engaged in the pursuit of new learning, the VIII of Pentacles may be a card of encouragement and reassurance that the energy you invest in your "apprenticeship" will be worth your while. Self discipline, preparation. Patience, productivity. This card suggests moderation, the Tree Of Knowledge, application of talents and success at hand which you have earned. All of these are implied by the VIII of Pentacles; purpose, small profits. improvements in work life. Training that brings both discipline and skill. It is a card of craftsmanship.

Eight stands for symmetries, structures, repetitive and self-sustaining patterns. Eight is the wheel of the year--and how many billions of years has this clockwork been running on its own? Pentacles represent the body, the tangible and practical. In a relationship reading, the VIII of Pentacles indicates that you are willing to continue the relationship to see where it takes you. You are prepared to invest time and energy into building the relationship. It is a card that indicates you are going in the right direction because you are working in a positive manner to make things happen. It represents using ones skills and personal interests to result in rewarding and profitable ends. For talented and enthusiastic people this is a great card. It also implies to have success you have to continue in a steady manner with no pauses or premature halts. This card also indicates a thrifty person.

Reversed

Reversed, the VIII of Pentacles is the recognition that proficiency is the enemy of innovation. The VIII of Pentacles is perfection in a self-contained world, a world that needs nothing but perfect pentacles, one after another. But what if the rules change? What if our artisan is called upon to sing opera? Short circuit. Syntax error. If you need to take a risk, or to shift gears, the VIII of pentacles can be a barrier card. It means you have to let go of the smoothness and predictability of doing what you've mastered, and be willing to make a Fool of yourself all over again.

When in reversed position it indicates that the Querent desires financial rewards but is lacking the ambition and will needed to get them. He/she is too wrapped up in everyday concerns and worries to take the time out to gain more long-term security. Instead most of the Querent's energies are wasted pursuing short-term gains and rewards. This card in reversed position may also act as a warning against wasting energies on short-term securities, advising to become more like the boy in the card. This card reversed also indicates that energy is being used inappropriately and skills applied for unsuitable and perhaps unscrupulous ends. When reversed this card implies dishonest dealings I business. This card also warns of short term profits at the expense of long term gain.

IX of Pentacles

Meaning Upright

The IX of Pentacles is caution and the ability to provide the situation and yourself with the security necessary to accomplish what is in your best interest. It indicates that you want to promote yourself and/or form a (new) partnership or alliance. A situation will arrive that will lure, entice or beckon you on - a very tempting offer. And your wish for a union will soon be fulfilled. Abundance. You need to be self-reliant, independent and free. Learn about your body and how Mother Nature provides all that is needed. Treat your health as your greatest wealth. ate. She is clearly a lady of refinement and grace, so it is incongruous to see on her left hand a bird trained to hunt and kill on command.

Nines represent personal integrity and completion, or the final stage of development. Nine is associated with the Moon - therefore dreams and delusions play a role in these cards. This final stage may bring certain problems with it, and past experiences and methods of coping become important here and are an intrinsic part of the meaning attached to the nines. In a reading, the IX of Pentacles indicates that you have reached a point in your life where you are feeling self-confident, and you are self-sufficient and able to rely on yourself. You have attained well-deserved success and may now enjoy money, leisure time, pleasure, and material comfort success and rest that is well-deserved. Appreciation is felt for what is now available, knowing that difficulties are over. This card denotes the ability to complete any work necessary through confidence in self-discipline and patience. The querent is in harmony with the nature that is around them. It is the luxury of leisure and solitude. It may also indicate your desire for these things if you do not already have them.

However, the IX of Pentacles can also equate to having all the material success you want but not necessarily being happy with it. The woman in the card does not look very happy, and the symbols of the walled garden, the bird (representing captivity) and the snail (representing something rotten nearby) indicates not everything being what it seems. Perhaps she is some sort of "trophy wife" who married a successful man who wanted a decoration rather than a companion. If this is the case, she is probably very lonely because she would be unable to associate with her husband or his friends, her servants, or childhood acquaintances either.

While she has everything that money can possibly buy, what good is it if no one will relate to her as a friend or equal? This card in a reading signifies the enjoying of success. It speaks of financial gains made from monetary sources such as gifts, winnings, inheritances and settlements. There is also a possibility of income from an unearned divorce settlement. This card can also represent depending on the spread popularity, common sense, and order arising out of chaos. This card can indicate melancholy because others think this person has it all but the person may feel something is missing. It can also mean buying furniture of fixing up one's home.

Reversed

In its reversed position, the IX of Pentacles suggests that you may be suffering from financial setbacks or experience a loss due to unwise decisions or foolish actions. Your foundations may be about to give way. If they do, learn from your mistakes and build a more solid and secure foundation next time. This card in reverse indicates a person who has obtained wealth from a deception. The reverse IX of Pentacles indicates someone who thieves, swindles and pilfers. Corruption and success earned on the backs and misfortunes of others. When reversed this card warns that the present calm and security may not last long.

X of Pentacles

Meaning Upright

Ten is the number between completion (nine) and new beginnings (1). It's like a spring board. The wealth has been secured, and it's that breathing space before you take your next step. Pentacles are solid, earthy, heavy, not emotional, inspirational or mental. Pentacles are the essence of the earth, and of manifestation in the "real" world. Shopping, eating, gardening, earning and spending money. The things that happen on the material plane that ground you. Combining these two ideals then, one can indeed say that X of Pentacles is about reaching that comfortable space where things have been achieved and rewarded and we have a time to breath before we start our next adventure. The X of Pentacles shows how family, or even extended family is important.

Traditions, safety in numbers, the wisdom learned from our elders. Being a part of something bigger than we are and realizing that the blood of our ancestors courses through our veins, and we are someone important. We're not just little insignificant' s lost in the world, we are integral parts of society and family. We are one. In a career reading, the X of Pentacles indicates that you would like a career that gives you a sense of completion, financial security and connection with others. From a numerology perspective, the tens represent the final stage where everything has fallen into line and you feel like you have accomplished your goals. Given this ten is from the suit of Pentacles, you are seeking a well-established career where you can be truly successful and good at what you do, and that will provide you the financial security you need to build a good lifestyle. You want to be able to provide for yourself by earning a solid income. Additionally, this ten speaks of family indicating that you want to be part of something bigger in your career and you want to feel connected to those with whom you work.

In a Celtic cross reading, position one, this card could indicate that the querent has these family issues on her mind. Issues of security, children, stability, blood-being-thicker-than-water type feelings. When we see this card in a spread it implies issues with inheritances and prosperity, like in family fortunes that are built up and handed down through the generations. It indicates financial and emotional security. It is a card that signals the formation of a family tradition. It also may indicate a good fortune via a dowry.

Reversed

Reversed, this card is about failure on the financial level. This card indicates financial loss, problems with investments, and lack of resources. Despite a lot of time and effort, there seems to be no foundation for future success. In some cases, this card represents the problems of money, such as fears about finances and quarrels over property, as finances become an impediment to the enjoyment of life. It could indicate that you are beset with financial burdens and responsibilities. In a relationship reading where the relationship is relatively new, the reversed X of Pentacles suggests that while you are keen to progress this relationship further, you are still not 100% sure that it has potential for the long-term and you may be questioning whether your partner is truly husband/wife material or not. This card reverse also signals the negative effects of vast wealth and the down side of restrictive effects of a long tradition. Family arguments over money. It can also signal breaking up of and estate after a death. The reversed X of Pentacles can also signal a burglary.

Page of Pentacles

Meaning Upright

Physical description - dark haired person. Young, even a child. Introvert. Tanned complexion.

Personality traits - hard working, practical and careful with money, but not stingy. Artistic, scholarly, enjoys material and sensual pleasure (but hasn't had financial success yet.) Conscientious. Sense of duty. Patient.

The Page of Pentacles, like the pages of all the suits, is a card of new beginnings, of inspiration and the initial stages of a creative project or venture. The young man is absorbed by the coin in his hands which represents his goals and dreams. Pentacles correspond to the alchemical element of earth. In this sense the coin may symbolize the beginnings of sensual awareness not only in terms of money and its value; but also in terms of a growing awareness of the importance of health and other material needs.

The Page of Pentacles is a card of dreams and the desire to fulfill those dreams in the material world. If you encounter this card in a reading, there is an indication that you may be in the midst of a new undertaking such as a hobby, business venture, or the beginning of a new educational experience. In any case, the page is a sign of enthusiasm and desire. He does not indicate the fulfillment of dreams as much as the initial motivation and energy to begin the process of creating those dreams in reality. This is a card of encouragement. Castles in the air may be beautiful in theory, but now is the time to begin to put foundations under them.

The Page of Pentacles can be used to identify an intelligent young person, a scholar, a young person who enjoys learning new things. When the Page of Pentacles represents a new event, this event will more than likely be concerned with the querent's material welfare. The page of pentacles has the desire to learn all things. He is dedicated to knowledge and the attainment of wisdom. He is devoted to all in which he is engaged. He has great concentration in his interests.

In a reading regarding spiritual issues, the Page of Pentacles could indicate a new dimension added to the querent's spiritual life. An event that will bring a certain richness that the querent hasn't enjoyed before. The Page of Pentacles could also indicate a new beginning of a material nature, such as a new and unexpected source of income, the sale of a project. Some readers interpret this card as meaning a change for the better. Pages tend to see only one side of a topic - and they're totally enthused with the prospects. Pages can be thought of as inexperienced -In a spread this is a meticulous hard working man. He is proud of his responsibilities. Basically he is honorable and a good administrator but can be a little diligent and overzealous with his duties.

Reversed

Reversed, the Page of Pentacles suggests we need to stop daydreaming about new things - perhaps it would be better to pay attention to matters at hand. When we see this card reversed it indicates to us that this person has no sense of humor what so ever and full of himself. This person likes to wield his power over others he feels is below him. Depending on the rest of the spread this card reversed could indicate bad news concerning monetary issues.

Knight of Pentacles

Meaning Upright

Physical description - dark haired young person, dark eyes.

Personality traits - takes action to make positive change. Committed to security. Hard working and responsible. Very serviceable person. Conscientious, yet dull. The Builder Of New Worlds.

Conventional, leaves nothing to chance, accepts responsibility easily. Trustworthy and steadfast.

The Knight of Pentacles is a person with the patience to accomplish all his tasks. He is reliable due to his sense of responsibility. If you are dependent on the efforts of someone else to help you accomplish some goal in life, they will prove trustworthy. This card indicates that you want the kind of personal fulfillment that only love or the grace of God can bring; and to enjoy the simple things in life and all they have to offer. Your efforts will be rewarded in more ways than one. This guy is active in a maybe boring but very persistent way. He is loyal and patient and will help you finish what you started, diligently. He is very much about fulfilling obligations.

This card signals that this is a impassive, indifferent and stoical person who does not always appreciate the feelings of others. He is very traditional, very clever at money affairs, patient and hardworking.

Reversed

The Knight of Pentacles reversed is about feeling stuck in a routine and a repetitive pattern of behavior. A relationship, job, family situation, etc. may become overly mundane and boring. To free yourself from this repetition, aim to do things a little differently each time and bring some spontaneity into your life.

This card reversed implies the person is greedy and grasping. They tend to be self satisfied and smug. It can also mean in reverse that your finances are at a standstill or a breaking point.

Queen of Pentacles

Meaning Upright

Physical description - dark haired woman. Large, strong constitution, cheerful. The ultimate mother.

Personality traits - she is secure, wealthy, enjoys luxury, and abundance. Generous and sincere, but lacking sparkle. Matronly. Good head for business. Sometimes moody, generally very caring. The Queen of Pentacles expresses practical energy.

She is the original Earth Mother. She's the one with the rows of home-canned goods on the shelf in the root cellar. She is able to work a full-time job, take care of the children, keep the house clean, and still have time to read the financial section of the Wall Street Journal. She probably has a little nest egg tucked away in a few bank accounts that no one knows about. Her style of mothering is practical. The punishment always fits the crime. Color on the wall? Here, take this wash cloth and clean it up. All done? Good. It's forgotten.

The Queen of Pentacles represents prosperity and security. The security can be either financial or physical. There will be generosity demonstrated and you will find freedom associated with this security. Want to establish yourself to yourself, to find your 'centre' or place where you belong, and for words (prophecies) or ideas to come to light. Keep following your star and you will get your wish. You may have to wait but what you want will come. You will be responsible for your own actions, and she will make sure of it.

This card can signal any or all of the following; she is pragmatic, sensuous, generous, abundance, practical, astute businesswoman, secretive, financially adept, good mother, nurturer, reserved, wealth, protective of her territory, endurance, stability, spinning and weaving, full of potential, power of prophesy, second sight, common sense, deviation, ancient tradition of earth magic, physically fit, strength, hard working, pleasures of the body, caring for and pampering the body, enjoyment of luxury, dignity, grace, prosperity, steadfast, good organizer, harmony, regality, devoted, affectionate, warm hearted, management skills, enjoying the fruits of labor, comfort, fertility, parenthood, love of all living creatures. Community life, takes responsibility willingly, love of nature, happy giving material help in demanding situations, shrewdness, ownership, steady employment, steady progress, evolution, voluptuous woman, material goods, all the good things in life, benefactress, emotional maturity, provider, philanthropist, display of wealth, practical wisdom, creativity, crafts, Great Mother, actions speak louder than words, confidence, down to earth, loves fresh flowers and good food, both feet on the ground, nurturer, a team player, family woman, tactile, indulgences, gifts, forgiving, firm foundation, sensible, environmentalist, bestower of life and bounty, unconditional love.

This woman is capable and practical in business. She can be happy either in the workforce or home. She does like her material comforts. She is responsible financially and shares her wealth with her inner circle. She is not however particularly bright nor insightful. She does however have depth of feelings and appreciates life's pleasures.

Reversed

The Queen of Pentacles reversed sees you becoming very consumed in your work. This card indicates that you need to rebalance your life, You may also find that you become a bit of a homebody and somewhat isolated from others you need to fight this urge and keep in touch with your friends and family as they will be a great help and support to you. The Queen of Pentacles reversed sees you feeling worried about whether you can be financially independent, while also still maintaining your family connections. You may be concerned that if you invest in your career or financial well-being, you might not have enough energy to invest in your family. Sometimes, you just can't do everything and you will need to make some choices.

This person pays to have the company of sycophants to shield her from criticism. She can neither see or rise upon material needs. This card in reverse indicates a woman with mood swings, highly changeable with a suspicious nature. She is narrow minded and doesn't take to things that are new or she doesn't understand. She uses her wealth for display and show of grandeur.

King of Pentacles

Meaning Upright

Physical description - dark haired man. Manager, financier, crafts person, businessman, farmer. Usually married. Mathematical gifts and attainments of this kind, yet normal intellectual aptitude. A devoted friend. Has considerable responsibility. Responsible and trustworthy. Slow to anger, cares deeply for family. Not very demonstrative, has quiet energy and purpose. Makes a vigorous opponent. Practical realist, considerable wealth, shrewd, yet unpretentious despite wealth. With Kings, the emphasis is on behavior. The King of Pentacles is not a real, many-sided person, but he does express an ideal of a certain type. In readings, he asks you to take the kinds of actions he might take. For example: keeping a commitment, fixing something that's broken, making money, or sponsoring a new enterprise.

The King of Pentacles is seated in the midst of his many possessions. To this King, it's not who you are or what you think or do that counts it's what you own. While he is an extremely hard worker, conscientious and reliable, and a great financier, this man has little in the way of imagination. He only believes in what he can see, touch, hear, taste or smell - anything else is highly suspect as far as he is concerned. He is a good provider, and an excellent husband and father, so long as his authority is not disputed. While basically good-natured, he wants to be King of his own castle and expects to be treated as such. He has high expectations of family members and may have trouble relating to his children if they do not think and act as he does. This is the sort of man who will automatically assume his children will one day take over the family business - that they may have other ideas will simply not occur to him.

When this King shows up in your reading, look at your life. What are you feeling 'stuck in a rut' about? Are you feeling like the Alchemist, or do you feel a need to transform some part of your life into gold? Is this another person, or do you think it's an aspect of yourself? Be careful not to get stuck in the mud. Having your feet on the ground is a good thing, but everybody needs to lighten up once in awhile and stick their heads in the clouds, even if it's just for a breath of fresh air. Although neither imaginative or intelligent he is dependable and loyal as a leader. He is trustworthy, patient and cautious and uses his inborn wisdom to create wealth. He is slow to anger but once he is he stands rigid against enemies.

Reversed

Grasping, dull witted, ignorant of art and beauty, bumpkin, dominating, materialistic, greedy, poor business sense, a loser, preoccupied with money, he who dies with the most toys wins, fraud, dishonest, rude, dogmatic, stupid, impractical, crude, workaholic, end justifies the means, every man has his price, stubborn, dogged, pornographic. This is a man who will do anything for money. He is impressed by other people's status and social position, and may be a snob to others while trying to carry the favor of those he considers above him.

Reversed this can be either a workaholic or an extremely lazy man who expects others to look after him financially. He may care only for his possessions, and uses other people to gain them. There is also a possibility of familial abuse, or he may be someone who marries for money, leaving the person only when he has gone through all of their resources. When we see this card reversed it is telling us that this man is easily bought, mercenary, very materialistic and dull. He is blind to beauty and hates change. You will find that it is very hard for him to adapt. He will stay on the same worn path even if it goes now where.

Chapter 8
Swords

The Spades in a regular playing card deck corresponds to Swords in the Tarot Deck. Swords represent the east or north, eagle, sylph, brown hair, brown eyes. They have to do with action, physical, working stages, change, force, movement, oppression, ambition, courage, trouble, and strife. They deal with the mental level of consciousness, thinking and intellectual. Swords mirror the quality of mind present in your thoughts, attitudes, and beliefs.

The suit of swords corresponds symbolically to the alchemy element of air (Aquarius, Libra, Gemini), the most ethereal element of the four. In this sense the swords represent the mind, the intellect, and rationality. In addition, the swords represent power and thus their two-edged appearance; intellect and power can be used for either good or ill and must be balanced by spirit and feeling.

Swords represent action, both constructive and destructive. Many of the cards in this suit are fighting or in states of misfortune. Sometimes this suit can also mean hatred, battle, and enemies. This is the suit of the warrior. Of all the suits, this one is considered to be the most powerful and dangerous. One can sense this by reading the above attributes of the card. Swords equals worldly power and sometimes violence.

Should the incidence of Swords be high in a reading, you may be quite correct to assume that the querent has many decisions or a decision has to be made. Also, there could be many arguments or even violence in his life at present. Don't be scared if a lot of swords appear in a reading. While swords represents a lot of negative aspects in a reading, swords serve as a warning to be careful and watch where you are going and to whom you deal with. That way we can use swords to our advantage and change things for the better.

The appearance of Sword cards is indicative of Winter or Spring, and months (as far as "time-telling" goes) in tarot reading.

Ace of Swords

Meaning Upright

The Ace of Swords augurs a new understanding of some issue that has been of concern, or the dawning of a new world view in the broader sense. The start of conflict or battle, cut to the chase, daybreak, new idea, seeing the light, first perception of the conscious mind, change, inspiration, original thinking, creative vision, discovery, force of life, moment of birth, cutting edge, pristine knowledge, illumination, transformation, communication, precision, raw power of the mind, free from restraint, cut through ignorance, first step, open mind, constructive power, fate, intuition, illumination, origin, enlightenment, progress, courage, power, keen intellect, glimmer of understanding, force of will, clarity, integrity are signaled when we see the Ace of Swords.

The Ace of Swords has the power of the King of Swords. The determination of the King is thus transferred. All that is endeavored will meet with success. Someone is going to express an interest in the work that you do, or have done...they could also express an interest in YOU. Conditions around the home front will be very tense and communication taut because everyone will be under some kind of pressure...so much so, that you will want to pack your bags and never return.

The Ace of Swords is often surgery or an injection, or the need to see a specialist. Clear thinking, clear the air, start at ground zero...that sort of thing. Think for yourself.

The Aces of all suits typically represent new beginnings or the inspiration of a new idea or feeling. This card indicates the eruption of a new point of view, the inspiration of discovery or intellectual accomplishment. If you encounter this card in a reading, there is an indication that your intellectual life is either receiving too much or too little attention. Though there is great value in the inspiration and power of the mind, intellect must be tempered by compassion and spirit for its true value to be manifested. The two-edged sword cuts deeply in either direction, and a fine line must be walked to achieve the balance necessary for a healthy life.

The Ace of Swords is a card of great power and is thus a sign that temperance may be necessary. This card signals strength, achievement, honest and ethics, judgment, self determination, championing causes, breakthrough, entrance of the knight on a white horse, release, new freedom, lifting of restraint, a beginning, breath of life, vitality, universal conscious, expansiveness, mind over matter, success, conquest, determination, triumph, determined, leadership, clear purpose, logic, reason, law, good judgment, decisiveness, center of attention, charisma, sexual vigor, fiery, cut away what's not needed , identify long term goals, dispelling illusions, lighting the dark places. The beginning of a conquest or victory. The birth of a child who could be a valiant leader. The ability to love and hate. When we see this card it indicates that someone is having a complete change of mind. It also represents the quest for total truth. It is a card of triumphs, victories and new beginnings. It can also mean the rebirth of something.

Reversed

When we see the Ace of Swords reversed its telling us there is present; willfulness, a bully, pushiness, powerlessness, helplessness and hopelessness. Its saying a person is victimized, threatened; that there are insurmountable problems, ignorance, confused, mental constraint, blocked, prejudice, tyranny, deliberate lie, verbal outburst, embarrassment, self destruction, disaster, obstacle, rejection. There are extreme feelings regarding the current situation and others surrounding you. Beware of trying to use too much power to gain an end. When we see this card reversed it is tell us there is confusion, exaggerated thought, violence destruction and the misuse of power. Depending on the surrounding card in the spread it can indicate a death.

II of Swords

Meaning Upright

The II of Swords represents the contest which is in stalemate. There will be no loser or winner. The situation may represent the coming to terms with situations and compromises being made. In any case, the peace is once again achieved. The person wants to move ahead without restriction, and wants a lover or romance. Expect a surprise in your business and personal affairs. The past is on its way out and a new element is about to emerge that will make the old way obsolete.

This is a card of choice, of the difficulty of indecision. The woman in this card is intentionally blinding herself in avoidance of a very difficult choice which must be made. Her avoidance brings her what appears to be a certain peace of mind, for she is very calm and seems somewhat relaxed despite the difficulty of her situation. Occasionally when we are face with difficult choices we attempt to hide from them and pretend to ourselves and others that if we ignore them long enough they will go away of their own accord. However, the decision will not leave us simply by our willing it to depart; the attempt to play at ignorance is not bliss. Our conscience will eventually force us into facing our refusal to deal directly with the situation.

If you encounter the II of Swords in a reading, there is the general indication that you are faced with a decision and that perhaps you are in a state of denial about the importance of your choice. Life's decisions are frequently quite difficult and raise the possibility of painful consequences, yet not to decide at all is a decision in itself. We must "take the bull by the horns" and make our decisions with our best intentions, fully aware of the possible consequences. The avoidance will ultimately only lead to a greater conflict in the end.

This card signals an alliance, a favorable friendship/mutual interest, suspending judgment, making peace, a choice made, a good time to resolve any outstanding differences. It indicates an end to pain (physically and emotionally) and end to quarrels. Balance. Friendship during adversity. A decision has to be made logically. A balance between equally matched opponents. A duel. Blocked emotions. Tension. Holding in emotions. Defensiveness.

When we see this card it is telling us either we have or need courage. It portends a situation that is delicate and in precarious balance against adversity. It does indicate that differences will be resolved depending on the rest of the spread. Depending on the surrounding cards it can also mean peace restored, a truce, a weight off of someone's mind and relief. This card indicates a decision has to be made.

Reversed

The II of Swords speaks in reverse of; release and movement in ones affairs but in the wrong direction. It signals lies, treachery, and dishonor are evident. When we see this card in a spread reversed it talks of treachery, violence, willful misguidance and misleading advice either given or taken as well as trickery and deceit. Reversed II of Swords indicates a Betrayal.

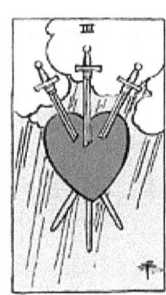

III of Swords

Meaning Upright

The III of Swords is a painful card, it gives that "twang" in your heart: loss, sorrow, mourning that loss. You know something painful has happened or surfaced from the past and that it needs to be cleansed.

The III of Swords indicates that the situation may become mournful due to absence or removal of something that is valued. The coming period will be full of opposition and delays. You want your lover to come back; or you have run out of hope or stamina and need to see results before you can get out of the doldrums or start some thing new. Abortive attempts or delays are in your favor. New ideas or actions will replace old ones, and something better will be established that could not have happened otherwise. This needs being taken care of before you can go on. It is no use starting on new projects; this card practically speaks for itself. It is a card of loss and difficulty, of sacrifice and broken relationships. It follows upon the difficult decision required in the II of Swords, where we are avoiding the necessity of making a tough choice. In the III of Swords, the choice has been made, and we are now experiencing the consequences of our action.

Often our choices involve choosing one good over another, or one evil over another, and thus when we've finally made our decision we are still left with the pain of losing the option we have not chosen. Frequently, however, the pain of losing something we once valued (such as a "comfortable" relationship in which we are no longer growing) is necessary in order to prepare us for a more fulfilling experience in the future. Absence. Sorrow. Disappointment. Strife. Removal. Dispersion. Diversion. Opposition. Separation. Delay. Betrayal. Abandonment. Rejection. A reversal of fortune. Sorrow, jealousy (unstable ground from beginning) reshape negative thinking. Disruptions. Heartache, ending of a relationship. Possibly a Three-way relationship where someone gets hurt. Acceptance of loss.

When we see this card we know the person is either feeling or going to experience great pain and sorrow. It can also mean that one has to use upheaval, destruction, discord and separation to achieve a positive end. This card like the picture indicates heart break, tears, strife and conflict. It symbolizes that something obsolete will be cleared away for better to come. From the pain something better is established.

Reversed

The reversed III of Swords indicates someone not willing to face the loss, and thus prolonging the pain. Denial of what is happening, so they need to turn the card around and deal with it. When this card appears reversed it indicates someone is going through spiritual and mental confusion. The pain begins to heal after the loss, loss is still present but the person is picking up the pieces. It represents a past loss, and depending on the other cards in the spread it can mean treachery and discord. Reversed this card indicates a broken truce, a war, quarrels and enmity. It also indicates mental and psychological disorder when reversed.

IV of Swords

Meaning Upright

This card, contrary to what might be its initial indication, is not a card of death. Rather, it is a card of solitude and the need to experience time apart from others to gather one's thoughts and feelings. Following upon the painful image of the III of Swords; the IV of Swords indicates our need to spend time alone to reevaluate our lives and situations. Solitude, although often difficult to bear, is necessary for us to be able to "recharge our batteries" and rejuvenate our spirits. Despite the fact that we often desire to get out into the world and interact with others to get our minds off our troubles, sometimes it is more beneficial to us to find a place apart and spend a little time by ourselves. This solitary experience always bears fruit in an experience of greater inner strength and confidence. If we are able to face ourselves directly and not run away from our difficulties we will ultimately become more alive and more aware of the good in our lives, and we will develop the inner strength necessary to cope more readily in the future.

The Four of Swords indicates a time when you can relax. Some actions may be abandoned during your retreat from the situation. The retreat maybe necessary to regroup your resources and conserve your energy. Your work environment will be very unpleasant due to tension you can cut with a knife. You will want to help or make amends with your family, but are at the end of your rope. This card could also indicate a death if other cards or categories support it. Time for resting and retreat. There will soon be a change back to the active life. Solitude and quiet. Need to plan and think. Rest, recovery, working on a problem. Renewal through truce. Hospitals and people who work in hospitals. End to conflict. Recuperation. A need to retreat from troubles. A peaceful interlude. Preparation. Withdrawal, even for the purpose of recovery, can shut a person off from the world, creating a kind of spell only outside energy can break.

When we see this card it can represent peace through arms depending on the spread. It is also a card representing rest after a battle if fought. It can also literally mean a tomb depending on the rest of the cards. And depending where it lies in a spread can mean relief from anxiety or sorrow.

Reversed

Reversed this card means renewed activity. Caution to use discretion in all one's dealings. May indicate social unrest, perhaps a short illness, or temporary financial problems, minor misfortunes may occur. Reversed this card can mean banishment, enforced isolation, seclusion, imprisonment, cowardice, depression and failure of nerve.

V of Swords

Meaning Upright

The V of Swords represents conquest. If you have been aggressive in your struggles, perhaps you will soon accomplish your objectives. If you have been passive, however, your interests may be the ones which give in to the wishes of the opposing force. You will feel that there are more obstacles ahead, and won't want to face the ordeal you know you must if you are to have what you want or the way you want it. You're in for a struggle and there is more work or problems ahead than you're aware of now. The V of Swords represents conquest.

If you have been aggressive in your struggles, perhaps you will soon accomplish your objectives. If you have been passive, however, your interests may be the ones which give in to the wishes of the opposing force. You will feel that there are more obstacles ahead, and won't want to face the ordeal you know you must if you are to have what you want or the way you want it. You're in for a struggle and there is more work or problems ahead than you're aware of now. The V of Swords is a card representing ambition in the negative sense. Too much ambition without regard to the consequences to oneself or others results ultimately in a situation of loss for everyone. You, the querent are coming to the Tarot for understanding, may be represented either by the callous winner or the dejected losers. In any case a negative connotation is encountered. If your focus is solely on winning your goals at any cost, you will eventually discover to your own dismay that the price of winning may not have been worth the reward.

This card shows a gloating and vindictive enemy taking the swords used in battle as the spoils of his victory. It often relates to a betrayal or sneak attack by someone the client trusts and does not suspect to be his enemy. It can refer to an unfaithful lover or a jealous person who sabotages the client behind his back. This card can also relate to vicious gossip and slander.

When next to cards relating to the past such as the V of Cups or the VI of Cups, it can mean the client still resents some slight he needs to forgive. Defeat. You need to learn about surrender and defeat. Failure, defeat, degradation. or conquest by unfair means. Cowardliness, cruelty, malice, empty victory. Tragic situation mourning. Smug and self-assured, the person the V of Swords talks about likes to stand out in a crowd. He probably is a very sharp dresser - at least when he thinks anyone might be looking. His hair may not stay as neat as his clothes, though, getting a little rumpled as the day wears on. When we see this card in a spread in addition to defeat it also represents; loss, failure, dishonor, a need to curb futile belligerence, accept the inevitable and swallow one's pride. It also speaks of negative attitudes and thoughts.

Reversed

The client will be cleared and vindicated of any misunderstanding or gossip. The enemy will be revealed as a vicious troublemaker and no harm will come to the client. This can also refer to the client forgiving past wrongs.

The V of Swords reversed can indicate conflict in your life that you have tried to walk away from but which continues to follow you. For example, there may still be an ex in your life who is making things difficult and who may be preventing you from moving on to new relationships. At this point, it is best to return to the IV of Swords and put some time and space between those with whom you have conflict, and allow for some of the raw emotion to fade. When we see this card in reverse we know that it can mean paranoia, indecision, malice, spite or someone acting as such in your affairs.

VI of Sword

Meaning Upright

There are times when we are forced to let go of something to which we may have been attached, and the process of letting go is frequently quite difficult. However, the sadness of the "loss" will ultimately be replaced by greater clarity, the calmness of the water in the distance, which will bring about a new understanding and a new acceptance of the changes in our lives. Often when we experience what seems to be sadness or loss we are actually only experiencing the "birth pangs" of a brighter future and a more peaceful experience of life.

The VI of Swords represents the dull, listless state that can come over us from time to time. When we feel this way, we don't even want to get out of bed. In readings, the VI of Swords usually indicates a period of mild depression. Nothing is seriously wrong, but nothing is really right either. You're getting by, but not thriving.

The VI of Swords may be a time of peace and relaxation after a long time of struggle. There could be a journey involved.

It will be necessary to apply all your energy toward the situation to get to this point in time. Problems with relationships, partnerships or personal property and want them to be resolved. The first step in correcting a problem is to acknowledge the fact that you have veered off your course, or are moving in the wrong direction and that recognition is enough to stop the momentum from continuing. Passage. You need to realize that you are now in a much better position in life. You endured a difficult transition and are now more able to deal with what may come.

This card is telling the person to change their beliefs about themselves, a trip will do you much good, journey, need for objectivity, moving away mentally or physically to view problems. It is telling of coming out of a difficult experience and that you cannot dwell on the past. "The load is light" - problems become more acceptable, easier to carry. Functioning in a difficult situation without attacking the problems. Travel. Movement away from danger. Travel in company. Being with others in same circumstances. Immediate problems to be solved. A positive direction to go in. Fleeing to safety.

It is also a card representing gradual change as well as movement from eminent danger and immediate difficulties. Depending on the spread it can mean the solving of current problems. This card can represent trips, a long journey to get away from something painful or obstacles that are overcome.

Reversed

When we see this card reversed it saying there is no immediate way out of present difficulties. A planned trip is postponed. You will stay where you are. This card reversed can also be telling us about unexpected developments in a situation, temporary relief from difficulties, need for continuing, effort and strength. It also implies when one obstacle is finished then there is another.

VII of Swords

Meaning Upright

This card is a card of deception and betrayal. It indicates the difficulty in life of trying to "get away with something." Often when we do something in secret, thinking we are safe and undiscovered, something goes awry and our secret is revealed to our embarrassment. The card therefore augurs caution and circumspection when attempting to use cunning to gain an advantage. There is no question that there are times in life when it is necessary to act shrewdly or do something in secret, yet it is these times when our conscience must be particularly active. In the long run, deception does not produce the reward we desired and may in fact cause much damage to our relationships and reputation.

If you encounter the VII of Swords in a reading, it is an indication that caution and wisdom are necessary in the face of a temptation to achieve gain by dubious means. Sometimes the VII of Swords means that you are running from something - commitment, responsibility, hard work, love. You may be procrastinating, letting problems slip because you don't want to deal with them. Sometimes we just have to face what has to be faced. The VII of Swords lets you know when you might be making things worse by running away.

An unwise attempt to take what is not yours. Betrayal of confidence. Plan might fail. Fleeing from your wrongs. Sometimes the VII of Swords means that you are running from something - commitment, responsibility, hard work, love. You may be procrastinating, letting problems slip because you don't want to deal with them. Sometimes we just have to face what has to be faced. The VII of Swords lets you know when you might be making things worse by running away.

An unwise attempt to take what is not yours. Betrayal of confidence. Plan might fail. Fleeing from your wrongs. It also means negotiations that are tricky. When we see this card it can also mean sudden desires and impulsiveness. It is a card of caution if you are facing opposition. It can indicate a change of residence or job or both. It also implies if one is cunning one can beat their opposition.

Depending on the other cards surrounding it; VII of Swords can mean no real progress, through lack of progress.

Reversed

The querent brings more to the situation than is required. A thief will return what was stolen from you. Possible wish fulfilled. It can also signify counsel and specific advice for a situation. This person shows reluctance to carry out daring actions when necessary. There is failure of nerve and reluctance to complete what was started.

VIII of Swords

Meaning Upright:

When we see this card it is telling us the person is feeling fenced in, restricted, vulnerable. It can represent too many ideas and no direction. It is signaling to handle difficult situations immediately. This card warns of gossip, advice, over analytical(back and forth) that one needs to pay attention. There are problems are behind woman. Your hands are tied but not your Legs are not tied; and the blind fold can be removed. Find out who put you in this situation, realize that you are not trapped, that you are free to move. This card represents restriction, a run of bad luck, feelings of being trapped and powerless. You need to use patient effort to get out of a situation.

Help is available if you ask. Restrictions will gradually fade. When we see this card in a spread its telling us that we are in a catch 22 that's keeping our hands ties. We are unable to act so have to ride out the storm. It can also imply jealousy from colleagues or family, a crisis or enforced isolation, illness and oppression and major circumstances dictate one's fate.

In this card, the woman stands bound and blindfolded, and surrounded by swords. It seems like she is stuck and it is hard for her to see what to do. Yet, if she could just reach out her hand, she would find that the swords are nearby and could be used to cut herself free. The swords symbolize our way of thinking about things they are both a cage and the way to let yourselves free of the cage.

Reversed

The VIII of Swords reversed indicates that you have come through a difficult time and you are becoming more open to change and self-acceptance. Reversed this card indicates that you need to free yourself from some of the limiting factors of your past. You have some skeletons in the closet that need clearing out allow yourself to let go of old patterns of behavior and belief systems that have previously held you back, and forget about being the victim.

The VIII of Swords reversed also suggests that you have been able to reflect on what didn't work last time and have changed your perspective and approach. This card in reverse also indicates your hard work is not reaping rewards. This person also is frustrated, depressed and feeling despair. The effort you are using is from the wrong place. Depending on the spread this card is implying change and liberation. Moving away from a problem rather than solving it.

IX of Swords

Meaning Upright:

This is the card of fear and nightmares, and therefore has an apparently negative connotation. However, the troubles portended by the IX of Swords are primarily of a psychological nature and do not necessarily indicate suffering in our external reality. Our experience of the world is greatly influenced by our expectations, desires, and fears. In large measure we are the creators of our own world, and our attitudes determine how we experience that world.

The IX of Swords indicates the paralyzing nature of our fears and negative expectations. If we allow ourselves to be bound by fear of the future we may eventually create a negative reality for ourselves by virtue of our expectations. Thus, the IX of Swords is a card which expresses an inner reality that may be "crystallized" or manifested in the external world if we are not able to overcome the negative feelings which affect us.

The IX of Swords foretells the arrival of conflict in your life. You may worry more about problems which never would have bothered you in the past. Other people will be opposed to your interests. The situation will cause you to be unhappy. Have been subject to prolonged periods of depression and are not happy with your present situation and want things to come together and work out. You will have good fortune later on. Time will prove to be advantageous and you will get what you want after all.

This card is telling someone to straighten out their circumstances. This card signals lack of sleep, guilt, depression and putting yourself down. To this person destruction equals way out. They are unable to see forward to positivity. When we see this card in a spread its telling the us that person involved in a love situation is suffering in some way. It is a card indicating cruelty, anxiety, sleepless nights, and of spite and slander which undermines confidence.

It can also indicate the kind of suffering which is eventually good, like treatment for a substance abuse. It speaks of Female health problems, possibly self-punishment and guilt, and mental anguish.

Since swords represent the mental realm, this card can be interpreted as mental anguish, depression, guilt, putting yourself down, nightmares, misery, a sense of hopelessness, despair, anxiety. This card represents the mind that injures itself through doubt or depression.

Traditionally, the IX of Swords has also meant sorrow for another person who is close to you. Along these same lines, the Nine could also mean worrying about a loved one, sometimes to excess. Keep an eye on the cards that surround or modify the Nine. If it falls next to the Star, remember that all is not lost. There is a ray of hope in there, a reason to pull out of the depression, a lifeline out of the anguish. If it falls next to the High Priestess, you must be prepared to face the truth without fear or doubt. In the same way, if it falls next to the Hermit, someone will show up to guide you out of the hole you seem to have fallen into. If there are aces in the spread, look for the light at the end of the tunnel, a way out in the form of something new and fresh. The astrological correspondence for this card is Mars in Gemini.

The IX of Swords in a spread implies deceptions that upset us tremendously, premonitions and nightmares, suffering and depression, cruelty, disappointment, violence, loss and scandal. This card represents the martyr who comes out anew after suffering.

Reversed

The Nine of Swords is all about worry, anxiety and not being able to sleep because your thoughts are running at one hundred miles an hour. Reversed, it indicates that you are putting yourself through the ringer, when really this doesn't have to be a complicated issue. The Nine of Swords reversed also suggests that your worry and despair may actually be causing you harm. The more you worry about something, the more likely it is to manifest into what your worse nightmares. Realize that life is not as bad as it seems and that the more you worry, the more harm you are doing to yourself.

You may also find that your dreams are very telling at this time use a dream journal to help you analyze what is happening at a subconscious level.

In reverse this card symbolizes distrust, suspicion, despair, misery and malice. On the other hand the IX of Swords reversed can mean that the person is letting go of grief and despair and moving out of a oppressive state of mind. Depending on the spread it can mean total isolation from comfort and help, institutionalization, suicide, imprisonment, and isolation.

X of Swords

Meaning Upright:

The X of Swords is very similar to the Death card of the Major Arcana. It is not to be taken literally as an indication of an actual death but rather as evidence of an impending change which may initially be difficult to accept. The IX of Swords indicates that there is finally closure to an outstanding issue, which may have been difficult to deal with. This is a card of endings and possibly loss, but as with all endings there is heralded a new beginning, a rebirth, and a rejuvenation of the spirit. We may have been struggling with a difficult decision for some time, or we may have been clinging to something, which was ultimately not in our best interests, and now we must learn to let go. The process of change is often difficult, yet life is filled with uncertainty; "The only thing constant in life is change!"

The X of Swords portends a difficult experience of loss or release, but a new awareness and a positive sense of relief that the difficulty is finally finished will eventually follow the pain of this experience. Though this card may seem negative at first glance, it is a card of hope and an indication that our troubles will not be permanent.

While the Ten of Swords appears to be a card of terrible misfortune, surprisingly, it often represents troubles that are more melodramatic than real. The man on this card has quite a few swords in his back. Wouldn't one be enough? Isn't ten excessive? Perhaps this gentleman's suffering - though sincere - is exaggerated as well.

One meaning of the Ten of Swords is hitting rock bottom. When one disaster follows another, we feel devastated at first, but eventually we throw up our hands up and laugh. It's so bad, it's funny!

When you see the X of Swords, know that the last bucket has fallen, and you can expect a turn for the better. This card can also show when you're in victim mentality. When you see the Ten of Swords, know that the last bucket has fallen, and you can expect a turn for the better. Ruin. You need to know that the worst is over. Though the hopes and dreams of the past may be dashed, new ones will arise in time.

If words cannot comfort, a wound this deep and loss this devastating may require professional help. The X of Swords depicts one of the most painful and sad images in the entire Tarot deck. However, despite the ominous images, there are positive aspects to this card. The sea before which the body lies is glassy and calm, and the sunrise is appearing in the distance beyond the mountains. The fire of the sun is burning the clouds of darkness away as it rises and the darkness will soon be dispelled.

When we see this card in a spread it means ruin, desolation and disruption usually in the form of a group. As the picture depicts this card in a spread portends sorrow, sudden misfortune, accidents, muggings or personal robberies. On the good side is that this is the worst of a cycle so things can only get better they can get no worse.

Reversed

Reversed the X of Swords is telling of fear of ruin, to such a point that emotional relationship/finances will not work out), ego-hang up, end of problem. It speaks of self-pity, doubt, betrayal and mistrust. If next to Ace of Swords, limitations are coming up. Hysteria, it would only take one knife to kill a man, yet this person has ten swords in him, even in his ear. When this card appears reversed it can represent an illusion of one's burdens and afflictions ending because the suffering will usually continue anyway. Also depending on the spread it can mean death and or a violent exchange. When reversed it can signal temporary good fortune as well.

Page of Swords

Meaning Upright

Physical description - Dark brown hair, gray/hazel or blue eyes. Deep penetrating eyes. Sporty, graceful, and physically well coordinated.

Personality Traits - May be promoting themselves, you should doubt their sincerity. They could be pessimistic, you must not allow their pessimism to "rub-off" on you. Quick witted, intelligent youngster. Eloquent and sharp. Eager to learn, adept at turning situations to own advantage.

The Page of Swords can also stand for a child or young-at-heart adult whose relationship to you involves truthfulness, ethical behavior, discouragement or matters of the mind. This relationship is likely to be troubled or difficult in keeping with the challenges of the Swords suit.

This card can indicate intellectual stimulation and excitement. As a child, the Page of Swords encourages you to have fun with mental activities of all kinds - learning, exploring, and researching. Enjoy the world of thought your mind can open to you.

The Swords, as we have seen in the card of the Ace, represent the element Air, and thus correspond to the ethereal nature of the mind and intellect. This card indicates the turbulent nature of intellectual discovery and inspiration unchecked by experience or wisdom.

The Page seems to be either on the defensive, hence protecting his ideas, or on the offensive, looking for some victim of the double-edged sword of his mind. Perhaps he is seeking a confrontation in the intellectual sense or has the desire to prove himself mentally superior to others. The Page of Swords is as perceptive as the Queen. He has the ability to find out the truth regarding all matters. He has both mental and physical agility. He is full of anticipation.

This is a card of ideas. You need to appreciate and communicate ideas, information and theories. Abstract thinking can help you see the weak spots in plans and systems. New information will produce surprises. Beware of gossip. Protect your privacy. When we see this card in a spread its telling us that there is a person who is a good personal emissary, that this card is associated with spying or surveying from a detached view point. It is associated with a person of grace and dexterity, one who is diplomatic, someone who has skills and one who has the ability to figure out the true nature of things. Depending on the spread this person is an expert negotiator for their peers. One of the true personality qualities of this person is their sense of detachment to things and people.

Reversed

Reversed, the Page of Swords can suggest you may be acting hastily, and without thinking things through properly. You may have a lot of energy behind you at the moment to get things moving, but the way you are going about it isn't quite right. Try to tackle things one at a time, rather than trying to deal with everything at once. This will lead to more meaningful outcomes. Your mind may be racing ahead of everyone and just confusing them all with your myriad of thoughts!

The reversed Page of Swords can also be all talk and no action. Take his promises with a grain of salt, because who knows whether or not he will actually deliver on them! The reversed page of swords indicates that this person is two faced, vindictive, cunning and not able to grasp on to something concrete. He looks for hidden weaknesses in enemies and is devious and snoops in other peoples affairs. Depending on the spread this card can represent unforeseen events, ill health or it can mean plans being overtaken by events.

Knight of Swords

Meaning Upright

Physical Description - Dark brown hair, gray/hazel or blue eyes. Tall, lots of charm and wit. Dark eyes. Lots of sex appeal. Charismatic, powerful, intelligent.

Personality Traits - Focused on making a point, committed to ideas. Very strong person. Initially helpful, but actually self-seeking. Makes a good friend, but a dangerous ally. Eloquent, confident, fast moving, easily bored. Breezes into life and then out again.

This card can indicate that the person this card represents can bring struggles or strife, which will cause you to stand up for yourself. A warning that own weakness can lead to difficult circumstances. He is a person who displays aggressive behavior.

The Knight of Swords is the gallant hero who is both strong and brave. He has great skill and is very capable of succeeding in all his ventures. You have established a link with someone (or something) and want the chain of events to continue. This is a very good time for embarking on new projects. Problems will be transcended or solved (whether they are mental, physical, emotional or spiritual) and you will attract whatever you need in the way of help or assistance. Ingenuity. You need to think of ways to turn ideas into reality. Develop your skills, ingenuity and self-esteem, or frustration and defensiveness will cause you trouble. Respond now with cleverness, outspokenness and foresight.

This card refers to a clever, skillful and active person who is courageous and strong. He is always at his best in a difficult situation. Depending on the surrounding cards this person has the tendency to dominate and he may be in or out of the clients life for better or worse. He is the archetype of a warrior.

Reversed

The Knight of Swords reversed indicates that you need to go it alone, even if you may make mistakes on the way. You are searching for freedom and independence, but may also be going about it in a very reckless way. When reversed this person is impetuous, sneaky, sly, deceitful, has little staying power but is fierce in action. This person does not finish what they start. Depending on the surrounding cards quarreling is possible. The surrounding cards may also signal that applications of great force and energy becomes simple minded indulgence.

Queen of Swords

Meaning Upright

Physical Description - Red head or dark brown hair, gray/hazel or blue eyes. Graceful.

Personality Traits - She has a fondness for music and dancing. She is able to speak on other people's behalf, but can also cause mental manipulations. Independent, rational, cool in a crises. Very alert to undercurrents, and should not be underestimated. Powerful intelligent woman. In a position of authority, she has the influence over the querent's ability to make decisions. She is probably separated, divorced or widowed.

The Queen of Swords represents the sternness of a mature intellectuality which is devoid of emotion. Mythologicaly, the feminine is associated with emotion, yet in this card the woman is stern and composed, obviously without much feeling. This card represents the intellect's ability to judge and discern impartially, without the influence of subjectivity or sentimentality. This card follows upon the rashness of the Knight of Swords, who lets his intellectual energy lead him into precarious situations. Intelligent, perceptive, penetrating mind, decisive, mature, competitive, independent, moral, sees a situation as black and white, virtuous, resourceful, respected, gets to the heart of a mater, candid, virgin, powerful and skillful communication, diplomacy and political astuteness, insightful, keen observer, knows how to confront, negotiate, and solve problems, organized thought, aloof, protective, dignified, wise, cold and calculating, unruffled, clear headed, detached, stern, scientific, uncompromising, disciplinarian, reserved, political consciousness, introspective, sound judgment, fair, articulate, accurately intense, exacting, hates to be told what to do, likes everything on the table before deciding, strong willed, ambitious, do the right thing.

This card signals pride in one's creative efforts, vigilance, dedicated to truth, calmness, determined, power of positive thought, bard and poet, quick-witted, confident, not happy in crowds, truth seeker, skillful analysis, gifted teacher, clear communication, straightforward, can laugh at him/herself, idealist, progressive, sees beyond the obvious, professional, humanitarian, secular humanist, hard to bluff, likes directness, stands up for what she believes in, a widow, can make it on her own, distant, advisor, no nonsense approach, well developed sense of humor, realistic.

This card depicts a complex, courageous intelligent woman who may have well suffered a deep sorrow or loss. She is very concerned with details and accuracy and is very skillful at balancing opposing factions to meet her own needs. She has attained inner wisdom and a sense of truth. This card is one signaling that a woman has overcome adversity especially at the hands of men and came out with a state of grace. This card also represents the ability that women have.

Reversed

Reversed this card signals a person who is weak, dull witted, doesn't get it, dishonest, speaks poorly, bitter, malicious, unscrupulous, intolerant, unreliable, devious, gossip, narrow-minded, short sighted, unreasoning, can't face the truth, no respect for rules, ruthless, without pity, frigid, sarcastic, bitchy, bigoted, petty.

The Queen of Swords reversed indicates that currently you may be thinking more with your heart than your head. You may be very emotionally involved in a particular situation or issue, but this may be distorting your perception of the situation at hand. You may need to use your head a little bit more to understand what is happening and read the signals more accurately. Try to purposefully look at this situation objectively and think with your head and not your heart this may give you a better picture of the situation and help you evaluate what you need to do next.

This card reversed signals sorrow for sorrows sake. It is a card telling of wrong doing in response to adverse conditions. When we see this card reversed it is telling us about a sly, deceitful, intolerant, narrow minded woman. She uses half truths and slander to make her points known. She is a formidable enemy when she uses her sharp but subtle wit and intellect.

King of Swords

Meaning Upright

Physical Description - Dark brown hair, gray/hazel or blue eyes.

Personality Traits - His application of intelligence has made his heart cold, and he holds back any subtle feelings. He understands human nature, and uses this understanding for his own advantage. In position of trust and authority. Logical and calm. He dislikes overt displays of emotion. Requires a lot of mental stimulation. Has authority over Querent's activities. Could be father, husband, employer, teacher, lawyer, doctor, professional advisor.

The King of Swords has the power and courage to accomplish all his desires. He is a symbol of power and superiority which may assist you in your individual quests during life. You will be fearful about your future and will want to see things more clearly, obtain a new perspective, or enlist the aid of a professional-type person. Stay detached and you will be able to perceive the truth in situations, and your impressions or perceptions will later be confirmed.

This ruler is the epitome of intellectual power and represents judgment, command, and rulership. His character indicates the stern leadership of a judge, lawyer, or military commander whose emotions must be kept in check under the pressure of battle. Indicates a challenging situation which could cause Querent to compromise himself. Advises caution. This card definitely represents a man who rules. He can be a law maker, someone with a rational, alert and attentive mind. He advocates law and order and being modern at the expense of tradition. He has a tendency to be over cautious and leaves one project quickly to start another. This card indicates a man of independent judgment and one who achieves what he sets out to do.

Reversed

Reversed, the King of Swords can suggest the misuse of one's mental power, authority, and drive. The reversed King of Swords represents manipulation, and persuasion in order to fulfill selfish needs. He is a very intelligent older male (or sometimes female) who likes to show off to others about how smart he is by using big words or talking about topics which nobody knows. He may also be very cutting in his words, critical of others, and stern in his manner.

This card may represent a person in your life or even yourself. You need to be wary of this type of person because, although he/she may be charming and intelligent, they can do only harm. They have only their personal interests in mind and will do whatever they can to achieve these interests, even if it means stepping on others. This card can also mean great disruption and contempt for those weaker than this person. This person abuses their power and authority. He is calculating and obstinate. He is capable of using ultimate evil to achieve his aims and desires.

Chapter 9
Conclusion - An Easy Spread To Get You Started

Now that you have enough basic information from this book you can start to use your tarot deck. There are many spreads people use the most common is called the Celtic Cross. But for simplification purposes I am going to end this book with a very simple spread to get you on your way to doing readings.

As you can see the tarot deck is very involved with meaning. I just gave the basics. This is to start you on your road to finding more information if you wish to pursue tarot divination. When we do a tarot reading you can see from the meanings of the cards that the relationship between cards in a spread can get very intricate and even complex for someone beginning to use the tarot.

The first thing to familiarize yourself with the cards that you can do as a daily exercise for yourself is to shuffle and pick one card for yourself every day. You can ask the deck what's going on today and pick a card. When you pick the card interpret the card based on how you feel it will fit your day. You just did a very, very, very, simple reading for yourself. After doing this until you feel comfortable you can now start three cards.

Three card spreads are very useful and simple:
1. Shuffle the cards
2. Focus on the Question.
3. Put one card in the middle. Depending on your question it can be the situation at hand. It depends how you want to use

the spread. If it's the present and you want to start from that point then that's the card that your day is starting out at.

4. The second card that you are going to put on the left side of the card at hand side is the past. This is what happened before the card in the middle. You can connect the dots how you feel it is relevant to you.

5. Next lay the third card on the right side of the middle card that's the future. It could mean that night or any day after the present.

You just did your first reading. When you feel comfortable with three cards you can go to 4. After you place the first card, for your second card you will place a card horizontally across it to make the shape of a cross. That represents any obstacle or thing that is blocking your situation. The card meaning on the left stays the same and the card on the right remains the outcome or future. You can also call card number one the situation at hand, and the crossing card the obstacle.

Like I said there are many spreads available. I find these are the best for beginners because it familiarizes you with the tarot deck without too many cards to interpret. There is so much information available for people today in relation to tarot cards that I hope this book inspires you to go on to become an adept tarot reader.

www.ingramcontent.com/pod-product-compliance
Ingram Content Group UK Ltd.
Pitfield, Milton Keynes, MK11 3LW, UK
UKHW022212230426
12048UKWH00016BA/794